D1397969

All About Houseplants

Created and designed by
the editorial staff of
ORTHO BOOKS

Editor
Marianne Lipanovich

Writers
Larry Hodgson
Susan M. Lammers

Designer
Gary Hespenheide

Ortho Books

Publisher
Robert B. Loperena

Editorial Director
Christine Jordan

Production Director
Ernie S. Tasaki

Managing Editors
Robert J. Beckstrom
Michael D. Smith
Sally W. Smith

System Manager
Linda M. Bouchard

Editorial Assistants
Joni Christiansen
Sally J. French

Address all inquiries to:
Ortho Books
Box 5006
San Ramon, CA 94583-0906

Copyright ©1982, 1994
Monsanto Company
All rights reserved under international and Pan-American copyright conventions.

1	2	3	4	5	6	7	8	9
94	95	96	97	98	99			

ISBN 0-89721-264-9
Library of Congress Catalog Card
Number 93-86235

THE SOLARIS GROUP
2527 Camino Ramon
San Ramon, CA 94583

Acknowledgments

Illustrators
Names of illustrators are followed by the page numbers on which their work appears.

Kirk Caldwell: 11
Ron Hildebrand: 7
Pamela Manley: 61, 63

Photography Editor
Judy Mason

Copyeditor
Barbara Feller-Roth

Indexer
Katherine Stimson

Layout by
Cynthia Putnam

Editorial Coordinator
Cass Dempsey

Proofreader
Barbara Ferenstein

Composition by
Laurie A. Steele

Production by
Indigo Design & Imaging

Cover Styling by
Michaele Thunen

Separations by
Color Tech Corp.

Lithographed in the USA by
Banta Company

Special Thanks to
Deborah Cowder
Dorothy and Jim Rice

Photographers
Names of photographers are followed by the page numbers on which their work appears.
R=right, C=center, L=left, T=top, B=bottom.

John Blaustein: 51B
Allen Boger: 37TL
Patricia Bruno/Positive Images: 6, 26–27, back cover TL & BR
Karen Bussolini/Positive Images: 9, 23, 34, 60T, 65
Kristie L. Callan: 38TL
Clyde Childress: 12
Richard Christman: 29BR
Spencer H. Davis: 37BRT
W. E. Fletcher: 37TR
David Goldberg: 32, 33, 48B, 50B, back cover BL
Margaret Hensel/Positive Images: 54
Jerry Howard/Positive Images: 4–5, 10L, 52–53, 66, 67, 71L, 99R
Michael Landis: 28, 51T, back cover TR
Lee Lockwood/Positive Images: 42–43, 75TR
Michael McKinley: 71R, 72, 73, 74L, 74TR, 75TC, 75BC, 75BR, 77, 78, 79L, 79TR, 80, 81L, 81BC, 82BL, 82R, 83, 84, 85BL, 85BC, 85R, 86, 87, 88L, 89, 90, 91, 92, 93, 94, 95TC, 95TR, 95BC, 95BR, 96TL, 96R, 97L, 98, 99L, 100, 101, 102BL, 102C, 102TR, 102BR, 103, 104, 105
Wayne Moore: 41TR
Jean R. Natter: 37CL
Ortho Photo Library: 8, 15, 30, 38TR, 38BR, 39, 40, 41CR, 41BR, 44, 45, 46, 47, 48T, 50T, 50C, 51T, 57, 70TL, 76R
Pam Peirce: 38BL, 70BL, 70R, 74BR, 75L, 76L, 81TC, 81TR, 81BR, 82TL, 85TL, 88R, 95L, 96BL, 97R, 102TL
Charles Powell: 41TL
Ann Reilly: 79BR
A. Rhoads: 41BL
Kenneth Rice: front cover, 10R, 13, 14, 18, 19, 21, 22, 24, 25, 29TL, 29TR, 29BL, 35, 49, 55, 56, 60B, 107
Malcom Shurtlett: 37BRB
H. B. Stowe/Photo/NATS: 1, 68–69
Lauren Bonar Swezey: 37CR, 37BL

Front Cover
A collection of houseplants graces this greenhouse window. With their bright light, greenhouse windows offer many of the advantages of true greenhouses, supporting a wide range of indoor plants.

Title Page
Thriving houseplants add a final decorating touch to any room.

Back Cover
Top left: Syngonium, coleus, and impatiens can be rooted in water.

Top right: New ferns will grow from spores in about a year.

Bottom left: Artful trimming removes brown tips without spoiling the appearance of the plant.

Bottom right: A potting bench for houseplants can be set up on a kitchen table.

All About Houseplants

Houseplant Basics

From the smallest child to the oldest adult, everyone enjoys watching plants grow and blossoms unfold. Their beauty and vitality are a source of delight. An indoor garden brings immense gratification and pleasure to the person who tends it.

To the beginning indoor gardener, and even those with some experience, caring for houseplants can be a mysterious and slightly disconcerting project. For many of us, the following scenario is all too familiar.

One day you go out to shop for groceries and the next thing you know you're in the checkout line buying a beautiful houseplant you just couldn't pass up. Welcoming your new friend into your home, you water it, set it on a sunny windowsill, talk to it, and then wait anxiously for it to grow and possibly blossom. Somehow, instead of bringing the lush growth you expect, all your tender loving care works awry: The leaves droop, the color fades, and any buds the plant has begin to drop. This dismal turn sends you into a mild panic—you add more water and fertilizer and cart the plant around the house trying new locations.

Your plant may well recover, but chances are that this random treatment, however well-intentioned, will not be exactly what it needs, and the experience will prove most unrewarding for you.

Just what are the best ways to keep a plant alive and healthy? Exactly what should you do for the houseplants in your home, and why? Watering, fertilizing, grooming, propagating, and seasonal care—often bewildering when first considered—are easy to carry out properly once you know exactly how they affect plants. For this, all you need is an understanding of the basic processes of plant growth and survival.

Houseplants fill a living room greenhouse window, taking advantage of the light and creating a pleasant addition to the view.

WHAT IS A HOUSEPLANT?

Houseplants are domesticated wild plants that have, over the years, been cultivated and bred to thrive in an indoor environment. Though they vary widely in looks and cultural needs, they have one essential feature in common—adaptability. They can endure the filtered light, widely varying temperatures, and low humidity levels found in most homes.

People around the world have been cultivating plants indoors for thousands of years. Long ago, the Egyptians, Assyrians, Babylonians, Chinese, Greeks, Romans, Incas, Aztecs, and countless other civilizations put plants into containers and brought them onto terraces and into their homes. During the nineteenth century, the Victorian English became enthralled with growing plants everywhere—in greenhouses and conservatories, parlors, bedrooms, and libraries.

People are still enthralled with displaying plants indoors, but no longer do we find homes decorated in the ostentatious, formal manner so popular with the Victorians. Today, we see kitchen windows brimming with potted begonias, or living rooms graced by ficus trees. Hanging baskets of grape ivy, philodendrons, and Boston ferns decorate many windows. And in interior spaces where sunlight never reaches, artificial lights provide life-giving rays for plants.

THE PARTS OF A PLANT

There are four major parts of a plant: roots, stems, leaves, and flowers. All are crucial to plant life and worth special attention.

The Roots

The roots serve two important functions: They anchor the plant, and they absorb the water and mineral elements that nourish it. Most of this absorption occurs through root tips and the tiny root hairs found on young roots. These root hairs develop in minute spaces among soil particles, where oxygen, minerals, and water are held.

Roots send water and nutrients to the stem to start their distribution to other parts of the plants. In some plants, the roots also store food.

Although they are not usually seen, the roots of a plant are crucial to its sustenance.

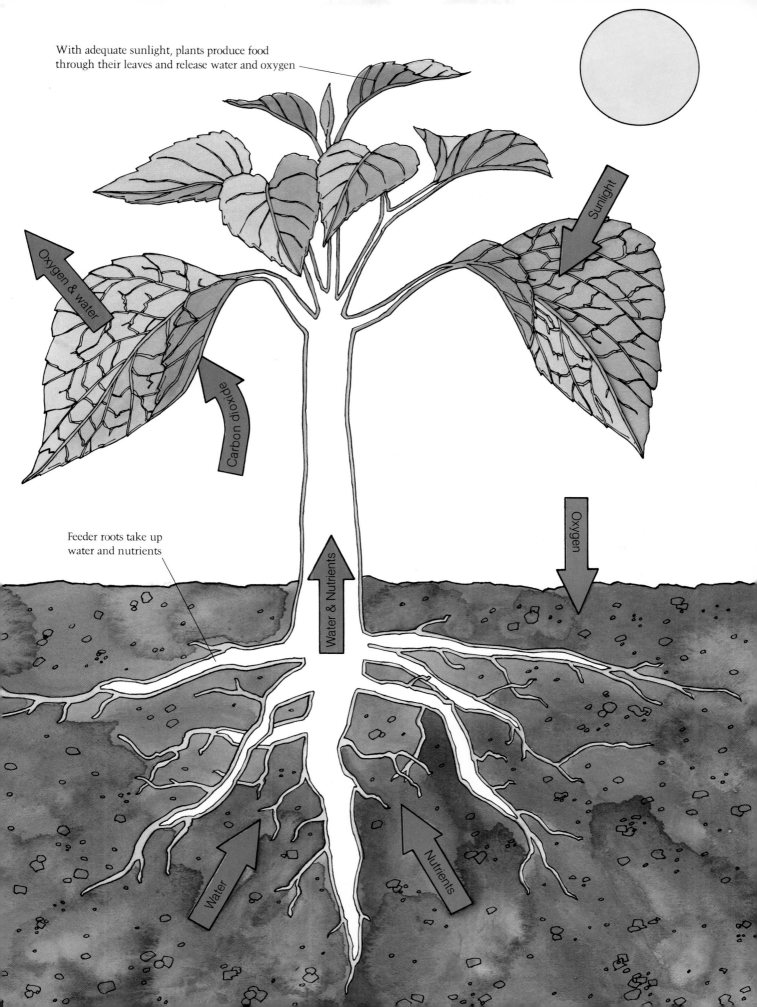

With adequate sunlight, plants produce food
through their leaves and release water and oxygen

Oxygen & water

Carbon dioxide

Sunlight

Feeder roots take up
water and nutrients

Water & Nutrients

Oxygen

Water

Nutrients

This arrowhead vine (Syngonium) is a victim of phototropism, the natural tendency of plants to grow toward a light source.

The Stem

The stem transports water and minerals to the leaves, buds, and flowers and distributes the food produced by the process of photosynthesis (see below). In addition, the stem physically supports the plant. The stem also stores food when unsuitable growing conditions prevail and through the plant's dormant period. In some cases, the stem manufactures food for the plant.

The Leaf

The leaf manufactures the plant's food through photosynthesis (see below). The large surface area and thinness of the leaf allow for the maximum absorption of light.

On the underside of the leaf are thousands of pores, called stomata, that expand or contract in response to environmental and physiological conditions. The surface area of the leaf and the action of the stomata let the plant efficiently absorb and diffuse gases and water vapor.

Leaves also can absorb minerals and other nutrients directly from the air or from direct applications of certain fertilizers, and they are crucial in the process of transpiration.

The Flower

The flower contains the plant's reproductive apparatus. The colors, shapes, and scents of flowers serve to attract butterflies, bees, hummingbirds, and other pollinating creatures. Although many plants will flower in their native environment, only some will bloom indoors. For more information on flowering plants, see pages 54 to 60 and the individual plant listings in the "Gallery of Houseplants," starting on page 69.

PHOTOSYNTHESIS: STORING ENERGY

Like all living beings, the food that plants actually use as a source of energy is sugar, but unlike other living organisms, plants themselves manufacture their own sugar through the process of *photosynthesis*.

In photosynthesis, light, chlorophyll, energy, carbon dioxide, and water act together within the plant to produce sugar and release oxygen. Plants harness the sun's energy to stimulate this process, and it will take place only when the plants are in the presence of light. What happens, very simply, is the following.

Plant leaves draw in carbon dioxide from the atmosphere and roots absorb water from the soil. The chlorophyll in the leaves and other green tissues absorbs the light energy and uses it to split the absorbed water into hydrogen and oxygen. The hydrogen and carbon dioxide immediately combine into sugar and the oxygen is given off into the surrounding atmosphere.

For photosynthesis to occur, a plant's leaves, stems, and roots must be healthy and interacting properly in an environment with adequate light, temperature, and humidity. It's especially important to note that this process is a plant's only source of food. Fertilizers are just supplements, similar to vitamins consumed by humans, so that no amount of fertilizer or number of applications can make up for any improper environment or care.

RESPIRATION: SUPPLYING ENERGY

Respiration is the process in which the sugar produced by photosynthesis is combined with oxygen and, in a sense, "burned" to release energy and heat. This reaction also produces carbon dioxide, water, and a small amount of heat, which the plant then gives off into the air. The plant uses the energy that the respiration process releases to maintain its life and produce new cells for growth.

In many ways respiration is the reverse of photosynthesis, and the same factors that encourage photosynthesis encourage respiration. In photosynthesis, plants absorb carbon dioxide and water, make food, and give off oxygen; in respiration, plants absorb oxygen, break down food, and give off carbon dioxide and water. Photosynthesis stores energy; respiration frees it. Photosynthesis takes place only in light; respiration is active both day and night because plants need a steady supply of energy. A plant therefore does its growing both day and night, whereas it is manufacturing food only during the day.

TRANSPIRATION

The heat produced in respiration can build up within a plant when coupled with warm temperatures. On a sunny day the temperature inside a leaf can be as much as 10° F higher than that of the surrounding air. Yet, plants must maintain a healthy heat and moisture balance to live and function efficiently. They do this through the process of *transpiration.*

Transpiration cools by evaporation. Similar to the release of sweat from your body, water vapor exits the plant from leaf pores (stomata) when they open to absorb the gases necessary in photosynthesis and respiration. If you have ever been in a forest on a hot summer day, the coolness you feel there is not only because of the shade, but also because water is being transpired by the multitudes of leaves that are all around you.

The rate of transpiration depends on the surrounding air's temperature and humidity. The higher the temperature and the lower the humidity of the surrounding air, the faster plants transpire, and the more water they give off. If they transpire more water than they can absorb through the roots, they will wilt.

Transpiration plays another crucial role in plant life. As the plant releases water vapor from the leaves, more water is drawn up into the plant. This produces the vital flow of water and nutrients absorbed by the roots throughout the plant.

LIGHT

Light is a critical factor in growing plants indoors. Without adequate light, plants cannot photosynthesize enough food for growth to occur. As an indoor gardener you should consider both the amount of light available and the length of time it is present in your home.

The *intensity* and the *duration* of light both vary considerably within a home, not only from room to room but also within one room. For example, light is less intense at a window with shades or curtains than at an unobstructed window. In the same room another

Different plants have varying light needs. By studying the natural light levels in your home, you can choose plants that will thrive in each location.

window may permit more intense light to enter, but for a shorter time.

Light at a single window will vary in intensity and duration if trees or other obstructions outdoors block the sun's rays at certain times of day. Furniture and reflective surfaces within a room can alter light as well. All of the conditions in your home that affect light should be taken into consideration when you set out to raise houseplants.

Most houseplants benefit from receiving as much indirect light as possible, rather than direct sun. Direct sunlight and the intense heat that often accompanies it can be extremely harmful to your plants.

Too little light causes a plant to elongate and lose leaves that it can no longer support. As the plant attempts to gather more light, the spaces on the stems between the leaves (called *internodes*) lengthen and the leaves grow broad and thin.

You can correct a low light situation in several ways. Increasing the duration of light helps compensate for low intensity, so you can simply move the plant to a window that admits light for a longer time. Or you can supplement daylight with artificial light (see page 13). If possible, move the plant to a sunnier window, or place it near reflective surfaces such as white or light-colored walls. In extreme situations, you can even place mirrors, foil, or white backdrops about the plant.

Too much light causes plants to wilt and their vibrant green color to fade. Young, thin leaves are affected first because they cannot hold much water. Inexperienced indoor gardeners often attribute the symptoms to a lack of nutrients. Before you rush to fertilize a drooping plant, check its light requirements and how they are being met. Excessive light intensity is most likely to occur at midday. Some plants may even wilt slightly during this time and recover later in the day.

Plants often grow in the direction of the strongest light source. You may notice that your plants appear to be "leaning" toward the

Left: This light-filled living room is perfect for sun-loving plants. Right: Placing these oak-leaf ivies (Cissus rhombifolia) *on plant stands moves them closer to the available natural light and also gives them a place of importance in the room.*

Sunlight at Various Window Exposures

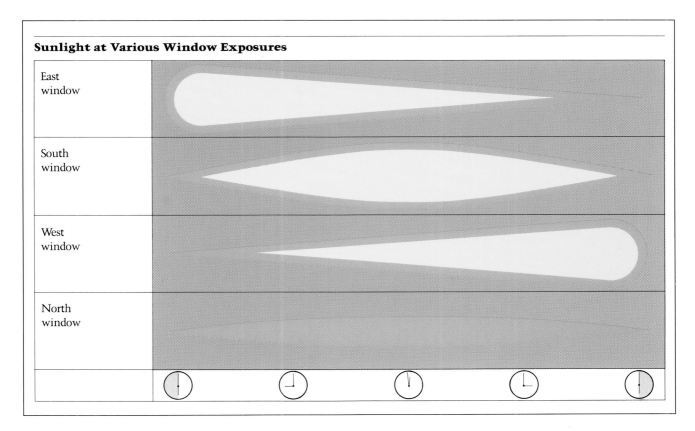

window. This is a natural process called *phototropism*. Rotate plants occasionally or provide supplemental artificial light so that they maintain a balanced shape.

Seasonal Light

During different seasons the angle of the sun changes, so that the intensity of light varies. In summer, the sun shines almost perpendicularly to the earth, striking it with maximum intensity. In contrast, the winter sun hovers low in the sky, even at noon. Its rays travel on a slanted path and consequently pass through more dust and moisture in the air, which scatter or diffuse the light, reducing its intensity. At noon on a clear day in midsummer, when the sun shines directly overhead, the level of illumination is much greater than it is at noon in winter. On a dreary winter day, the light intensity at the same location may be only one-twentieth the intensity level in summer. Given this reduced intensity, it's easy to understand why so many plants grow very slowly during the colder months of the year.

Where you live also affects how much light you receive. For example, sunlight in mountainous areas during winter is much more intense than in low-lying locations because the

higher elevation means thinner air and less light diffusion through the atmosphere. In winter, the sun rises and sets farther to the south of the Northern Hemisphere. Consequently, tropical and subtropical climates receive more bright light than those in extreme latitudes.

Even within your local area, light intensity will vary, and not just because of the seasons. Smoke from a local industry may make sunny days hazy. Clouds or fog cut down light. Trees and shrubs that shade your home reduce the amount of light that passes through your windows. Screened windows, doors, or porches reduce light by as much as 30 percent. A white house next door or a light-colored cement driveway will reflect sunlight, increasing the intensity of light your rooms receive. Snow reflects a great deal of light, especially on a sunny day.

All of the care you give your plants must also coincide with the seasonal increases and decreases in light intensity. During the summer, when light is brightest and heat is highest, all plant life processes speed up and plants absorb more water, more minerals, and more carbon dioxide. Therefore, you must provide them with more moisture and fertilizer. During the winter, when light is less intense and

Most flowering plants, such as these hyacinths, generally prefer full sun.

photosynthesis slows, a cutback in moisture and fertilizer is in order.

Light Categories

To establish some good general guidelines for assessing the light situations in your home and selecting plants to fit them, carefully read the following descriptions of the light exposure categories for indoor plants. Apply these criteria to various locations within your home and try to choose plants that will do well in them.

Full sun Locations that receive as much light as possible, generally more than four to five hours of direct sunlight daily, are in full sun. Such a location can be found within 2 feet of an unshaded south-facing window. Very few plants other than cacti and some succulents will survive the heat in this setting in summer.

Some direct sun Areas that are brightly lit but receive less than five hours of direct sunlight during the day, usually in the morning or afternoon, receive some direct sun. Windowsills facing east or west and locations at least 2 feet but not much more away from a south-facing window usually fit this category. Some protection from intense summer sun is usually necessary in west-facing windows. These locations

are ideal for many flowering houseplants and some foliage houseplants.

Bright indirect light This is an all-purpose light level at which most houseplants survive. These locations receive as much light as possible without any direct sun. They can be found within 5 feet of a window that receives direct sun for only part of the day or a northeast or northwest window that receives a few hours of early morning or late afternoon sun and is well lit the rest of the day. You can also create the same effect in sunnier windows by drawing curtains or shades during the sunniest part of the day or by moving plant locations back from the window. Most foliage plants prefer this setting.

Moderate light This is average indoor light. It can be found between 5 to 8 feet from an east- or a west-facing window that receives direct sun part of the day or in front of a north-facing window. Areas near sunless windows can also fit this category. Few flowering plants will bloom in this light level, but a fair number of foliage plants will adapt to it.

Low light Locations that are poorly lit or in light shade are low-light areas. These positions are generally far from windows that receive direct sunlight. Only a few plants will tolerate such conditions.

Artificial Light

The use of artificial lighting makes it possible to grow plants in places that otherwise would be out of the question. It provides you with a constant and dependable source of light that will encourage health and bloom, let plants flourish in out-of-the-way or difficult places, help transform dark areas into attractive plant displays, and pull your plants through long periods of cloudy weather that would otherwise inhibit growth.

Choices in artificial light have changed greatly over the past few years. Now you can choose among incandescent, fluorescent, and halogen lights.

Before choosing a plant light, it is important to learn how light rays, or wavelengths, affect plant growth. Light can be broken down into different wavelengths, which are perceived as colors. Although it is believed that plants make use of all light waves, the most necessary to plant life are those at the ends of the spectrum, red and blue to violet. Red rays stimulate flowering and affect other growth processes, including stem length and leaf size. Blue and violet rays promote foliage growth. And both red and blue light waves play important roles in photosynthesis.

Incandescent lights Because most homes today are lit by incandescent light, incandescent bulbs are cheaper and simpler to install than fluorescent lighting. However, they have some serious drawbacks for plants: They project light that is not evenly distributed; they are relatively inefficient, requiring more energy to produce light and also frequent replacement; and they emit mostly red light waves and lack enough blue light waves to meet plant needs. Even special incandescent plant lights

A piggyback plant (Tolmiea menziesii) *receives added light from the incandescent lamp next to it.*

A halogen lamp, with its clear beam of light, draws immediate attention to the century plant (Agave americana) *it illuminates.*

tend to be weak in blue rays. Incandescent lights also generate heat that can dry the surrounding air and even scorch plants. (Unlike regular incandescent lights, incandescent plant lights reflect heat away from the plant.) Incandescent light is best used as supplemental light in areas where plants receive some natural light.

Fluorescent lights　There are several advantages to choosing fluorescent bulbs. Despite a higher initial cost and more complicated installation procedures, they are more economical in the long run because they produce more light with less energy. (A fluorescent tube produces 1½ to 3 times as much light as an incandescent bulb of the same wattage.) They also produce

less heat, and they produce light over a greater range of the spectrum, and mostly in the blue range. Fluorescent lights work well in areas where there is no natural sunlight.

Full-spectrum fluorescent plant lights give off a more perfectly balanced light quality than ordinary fluorescent lights. Use full-spectrum fluorescent plant lights for plants that will not do well under ordinary cool-white or warm-white fluorescent tubes, such as some orchids, as well as on plants that prefer full sun.

Halogen lights　Currently fashionable in homes and offices, halogen lights give off light of exceptional quality, making them good choices for lighting indoor plants. They also dramatically draw attention to the plants they illuminate with their clear, intense light. However, they give off a great deal of heat and will burn the leaves of plants that are too close. Because halogen lamps produce beams that are quite narrow, they are best for illuminating individual plants or small groups of plants.

TEMPERATURE, HUMIDITY, AND AIR CIRCULATION

All of the elements of a plant's environment must be in balance to ensure continuing health and growth. Three important elements in maintaining this balance are proper temperature, humidity, and air circulation.

Temperature directly affects plant metabolism. Most plants we grow indoors adapt to the temperatures normally found in our homes, around 70° F days and 65° F nights. At night, almost all plants benefit from at least a 5° F drop in temperature. This gives them a breather from the rapid rate of transpiration during the day. Overnight any water deficit in the leaf cells is corrected as roots take up water.

If you assume that your house or apartment temperature is uniform, you are likely to be in for a surprise. Generally variations occur even within each room. Use a thermometer to check the temperatures of different locations in your home throughout the day.

Seasonal temperature changes must also be taken into account. Winter temperatures in particular vary widely due to home heating and the cold air that enters the house at windows and doors. Seasonal changes can be sudden and severe enough to warrant moving a plant to a new location, especially if it's growing on a windowsill.

Tropical plants that are native where temperatures and humidity are high, such as flame-violet (*Episcia cupreata*), fishtail palms (*Caryota*), and some ferns, may do best near a window in a room with an appliance that vents moist heat, such as a dishwasher, a clothes dryer, or a humidifier.

Cool-loving plants (55° to 60° F days and 50° F nights), such as cyclamen and some orchids, do well in rooms where indirect sun keeps temperatures low.

The moisture content of the air is called humidity. Expressed as relative humidity, it is a percentage of the maximum amount of water vapor the air can hold at a given temperature.

Nearly all houseplants prefer a humidity level of 50 percent or higher; however, in drier climates it is practically impossible to create this level of humidity in a home. As a result, many houseplants suffer from low humidity. This is especially true in winter, when dry home heating robs the air of moisture. At this time of year, humidities of 4 to 10 percent are common. Electrical heating systems dry out the air more than hot-water heating systems.

Adding a layer of moss around the base of a plant and keeping it moist helps boost the level of humidity.

A cool vapor humidifier is one excellent way to increase the humidity in your home. Portable units can be placed wherever they are needed. Or you may want to have a humidifier installed as a part of your home's central heating system. Such systems should have the capability of raising the humidity by 25 to 30 percent, even on the coldest winter days.

The simplest method for humidifying the air around plants is to set pots in a saucer or tray filled with pebbles, perlite, or vermiculite, called a humidifying tray or a pebble tray. Fill the tray with enough water so that it reaches just below the surface of the pebbles or potting mix, being careful not to add so much that the bottom of the pot touches the water (or else the roots may rot). As the water evaporates it fills the surrounding air with moisture. Be sure to add water to the tray as it evaporates.

Also, if plants are grouped together rather than separated, the leaves will catch and hold transpired moisture. Leave enough room between plants to allow some air circulation and discourage fungus disease from forming.

Another popular method for increasing humidity, especially for orchids or ferns, is misting. The spray from a mister should create a fine cloud of moisture. Mist in the morning to early afternoon so that the moisture evaporates before nightfall. Leaves that are moist for long periods are more prone to disease. Fuzzy-leaved plants, such as African violets (*Saintpaulia*), should not be misted; they'll develop permanent water spots if the tops of the leaves become wet.

Misting, unless done several times a day, only temporarily raises the humidity around plants. If the room humidity is low, the moisture will evaporate quickly. Humidifying the air and keeping plants adequately watered are the only ways to ensure that they have sufficient moisture.

Air circulation is as important to plants as it is to people. Soft breezes of warm, humid air supply necessary oxygen and moisture. When plants are cramped together so that air cannot circulate among them, or are placed in an environment that lacks circulation, fungus disease is much more likely to occur.

At the same time, drafts or the movement of dry air over leaves can cause moisture stress and leaf burn, especially in direct sun. Sudden changes in air movement and temperature do not benefit plants, either. These can send plants into shock. Be careful if you keep your plants near a window, especially during winter, when cold drafts and frosted window panes can cause great harm.

Pollutants in the air can also harm plants. Fumes from burning propane or butane gas are likely to cause flowering plants to drop their buds. They can also cause leaves to yellow and drop off. Fumes from burning natural gas are not harmful to plants.

GETTING STARTED WITH HOUSEPLANTS

Initially a new plant will require more than a simple day-to-day care routine. Special tasks such as supplying nutrient-rich potting mix, repotting into suitable containers, or arranging plants in hanging containers or terrariums will have to be done early and with care to ensure that your plants have the best chance at long-lasting health and beauty.

An important key to a vigorous, long-lasting indoor garden is to start out with the healthiest plants you can find. Look at your purchase as an investment: Take the time to find out where you can get the best plants for your money, and most importantly, always examine them carefully before you buy.

Buying plants in spring or summer is best; they adapt to new surroundings much more quickly at that time. In fall, plants are beginning to enter their dormant period and will not adjust as well.

When buying plants, carefully examine all the plants on display before deciding. Selecting the right plant means more than just buying the first plant that catches your eye. You need to consider where you want to place the plant and if that location will fit the plant's needs for light, temperature, and humidity levels.

You also need to consider the care the plant requires: If you are a novice gardener or have an erratic schedule, you may want to stay away from such hard-to-grow plants as orchids and weeping figs (*Ficus benjamina*). Here are a few points to heed when buying plants.

• Watch for brown edges on leaves or evidence that edges have been trimmed away.

• Large gaps between new leaves suggest that heavy doses of fertilizer have been applied to induce rapid growth, or that the plants have been held too long in inadequate light.

• Inspect the leaves and the junctures of stems and leaves for any signs of insects or disease. This is very important, because if these problems sneak into your home on a new plant, they can spread to your entire collection. Even if the plant seems free of pests and diseases, you should isolate it for up to two weeks when you get it home to keep any unnoticed problems from affecting your other plants.

• Flowering plants, with few exceptions (see the individual listings in the "Gallery of Houseplants," on page 69), should have lots of buds just ready to open. If they are already blooming, much of their beauty may already be spent.

• Check any supporting stakes or screens to make sure that they are not hiding broken stems, branches, or trunks.

• If the weather is cold, be sure that the plant is wrapped well before you take it outdoors. In summer, do not leave plants for too long in a hot car; the sun shining through the windows will quickly burn them. At any time of the year, try to return a houseplant to a sheltered environment as quickly as possible.

When you bring a new plant home from the store, it will need to adjust to its new surroundings. It may even go through a mild case of shock. In a very short time it has traveled from the meticulously controlled environment it enjoyed in the commercial greenhouse, to the retailer, and finally to a home with reduced light, lower humidity, and fluctuating temperatures.

This acclimation period will take a few weeks. In the first week leaves may yellow and blossoms may drop. During the acclimation period try to pay special attention to the plant's needs. If you have chosen a plant that tolerates low light conditions, remember that it probably

Caring for Gift Plants

Not all potted flowering plants were intended as permanent houseguests. Many, including such popular ones as chrysanthemums, cinerarias, and poinsettias, are specifically grown and sold as temporary indoor decorations, to be discarded after their flowering has ceased. Some of these gift plants, however, can continue to be grown indoors and will rebloom with the proper care.

Commercially, gift plants are grown in cool greenhouses, which gives a clear hint as to their needs. For a maximum blooming period, it is important to re-create the cool conditions in which they normally grow. Place them in a cool room (55° to 65° F) at night and keep them out of direct sun while they are in full bloom.

After blooming ceases, pinch or cut off the faded flowers. Put the plants in the brightest possible spot in the home, shielding them only from direct midday sun, and fertilize them regularly to build up their strength. Some, such as chrysanthemums and poinsettias, should be pinched back regularly throughout the summer to keep them compact.

Most gift plants are best placed outside for the summer. When all danger of frost is past, move them outdoors to a shady spot and gradually acclimate them to stronger and stronger light over a 2-week period until they can take partial sun without burning. The pots can either be sunk into the ground or placed on a balcony or terrace. Careful watering and regular fertilizing will be necessary throughout the summer. In warmer climates, gift plants can simply be planted permanently in the garden.

In early fall, when evenings are cool but before the first frost, bring tender varieties back indoors and place in a cool spot (between 45° and 65° F). No fertilizer will be necessary at this time, and watering can be moderate, since the plants will be semidormant. When the flower buds begin to change color, the plants can be given warmer temperatures and enjoyed as flowering plants.

Some varieties need a few weeks of short days in order to bloom. These include chrysanthemums, poinsettias, and Rieger begonias. Starting in October, put them in a dark location from 6 o'clock in the evening until 8 o'clock the next morning, taking care that no light reaches them. Regular lighting can be resumed once the buds begin to show color.

Most gift plants, including azaleas, caladiums, amaryllis, holiday cactus, cyclamen, poinsettias, kalanchoes, German and Chinese primroses, and Jerusalem cherries, will rebloom well when treated as above. A few, including bulbs such as daffodils, tulips, and crocus, as well as miniature roses and polyanthus primroses, can be safely planted outdoors on a permanent basis in all but the coldest climates and are, in fact, best grown that way. In climates where temperatures do not drop below freezing for long periods, hydrangeas, Easter lilies, gardenias, and chrysanthemums also can be planted outdoors. Finally, calceolarias, cinerarias, fairy primroses, and ornamental peppers are best treated as annuals.

has been grown in strong light and needs time to adjust to the change in light intensity. If possible, make the change gradual by placing the plant in one or two interim locations with decreasing light intensity for at least a month in each spot. Finally, place the plant in the chosen site and give it a few weeks to begin actively growing again. If it doesn't grow or steadily declines, a brighter location may be the answer.

Keep plants moderately moist during this adjustment period. Water thoroughly, then discard the excess water from the drainage saucer. Once a plant is in its permanent location, try to keep the surrounding environmental factors consistent.

TOOLS

Using the right tools will make your indoor gardening job much easier. It's a good idea to have several sizes of pots at hand and, for rooting cuttings or planting seeds, some plastic flats.

Equip yourself with a good pair of sharp shears or scissors and a sharp knife for dividing plants and removing them from pots. Shears are available in several sizes, from the standard down to small needle nose shears for delicate work.

A watering can with a long spout obviously will be useful, and brushes, sponges, or soft rags will serve to clean off the dust and grime that collect on large leaves, clogging air passages and dulling their sheen.

To closely assess temperature conditions in your home, a thermometer that records both maximum and minimum temperatures will prove useful. Another instrument that can be quite valuable is a *hygrometer,* used to measure relative humidity.

Most garden centers also stock inexpensive light meters. Light meters indicate whether the light in a particular spot is low, moderate, or high. The readings are not scientifically exact, but they are accurate enough to let you choose a suitable plant for that location.

Moisture meters are similarly helpful. They measure the presence of electrolytes or fertilizer salts in the soil. Since water carries the electrolytes, a high reading ordinarily indicates the presence of moisture. After awhile, however, as salts build up in the soil, the meter will give less accurate readings.

Spraying a plant with a mister temporarily increases the humidity around it. More important, misting washes grime from the leaves, helps control pests, and makes a plant look healthy and cared for.

If you plan to take any cuttings, some rooting hormone will be helpful. It's good to keep some liquid fertilizer handy as well. A few broken

The proper tools will make caring for your houseplants a pleasure, not a chore.

pieces of clay pot, a circle of plastic window screening, or a piece of old nylon stocking will serve to cover drainage holes and keep the potting mix from flowing out the bottom of containers. A spray bottle for applying chemical controls is also handy. Be sure to label spray bottles clearly, and don't store them until they are empty and clean.

Other tools that are popular with home gardeners are plastic wrap for layering plants, plastic labels for labeling plants, a spoon for repotting and dispensing fertilizer, and a watering wand and a squeeze bottle for watering hanging plants.

CHOOSING A POTTING MIX

The medium in which a plant grows serves three main purposes: It acts as a support, keeping the plant from falling over; it stores water and nutrients; and it provides sufficient air circulation to keep the roots well oxygenated. Any potting mix that supplies those three basic needs will give good results.

Today's potting mixes often contain no true soil at all; they go under the name *peat-based mixes* or *soilless mixes*. Typically they are composed of peat moss or some other partially decomposed plant material, such as fine fir bark, and inorganic elements such as perlite and vermiculite. They offer all the qualities that garden soil offers outdoors: They provide good support for roots and excellent retention of water and minerals; and they are also quite porous, allowing easy circulation of oxygen. Their chief disadvantage is that they are almost totally lacking in any natural nutrients, so that plants will not thrive unless small amounts of fertilizer are added, preferably with each watering. Also, since even the best soilless mix becomes compacted with time, it needs to be replaced every year or so.

Another important aspect of soil is its acidity or alkalinity. This is measured by the *pH* scale, which runs from 0 to 14, with 7 being neutral. A pH reading higher than 7 is on the alkaline side; a reading less than 7 is on the acid side.

Different plants have different pH preferences, but most plants we grow indoors prefer a slightly acid soil with a pH between 6.5 and 7. A highly alkaline soil will cause a plant to lose leaf color and will stunt its growth. Highly acidic soil produces wilting and dropping leaves. If you have reason to believe that pH is

a problem with your plants, you can test the soil yourself with one of the inexpensive kits commonly available at garden centers.

Most prepackaged mixes are slightly acidic; they have a pH of about 6.5 to 6.8. The mixes suggested here include dolomitic lime (also sold under the name "Dolomite") to raise the pH to a similar level. For acid-loving plants (azaleas, gardenias, citrus, and so on), prepare the mixes without the dolomitic lime. Many cacti and succulents prefer a neutral or slightly alkaline soil, which you can easily provide by adding extra lime.

Preparing Your Own Potting Mix

Unless you have a place to prepare potting mixes, time to do the work, and a source of ingredients, it is easier to buy ready-to-use mixes. There are many brands available and some are far superior to others. Ask for recommendations from the staff at your local nursery or plant store.

Make sure that the mix is appropriate for your plant and that it's light enough to provide adequate drainage and root aeration. If prepackaged mixes do not drain well, you can lighten them with organic amendments or with perlite, pumice, or vermiculite. Adding organic amendments such as peat moss, ground bark, manure, leaf mold, or compost will improve any mix.

If you do prepare your own mix, the following basic recipes should meet your needs. The ingredients for a homemade houseplant mix are the same as those found in commercial mixes. Below are listed some common ingredients in

Potting mixes are designed to meet the needs of different types of plants. Shown left to right are mixes for an orchid, a standard houseplant such as a coleus, and a cactus.

potting mixes. Each plays a specific role in helping houseplants grow and flourish.

Garden soil or garden loam　Many growers like to add some garden soil, also called garden loam, to soilless mixes. It makes the mix heavier, providing tall plants with more support, and it contains certain nutrients. You can buy an already pasteurized mix containing garden soil or use your own garden soil.

If you use soil from the garden, you must sterilize it to eliminate harmful organisms, weed seeds, and pests. The process is easy: Moisten small quantities of the soil and place it in a covered container in the oven at 200° F. Insert a thermometer in the soil and keep its temperature between 150° and 180° F for 30 minutes. You can also pasteurize potting mix in a microwave oven. Place the moist mix in a damp container whose depth is less than 3 inches. Turn the microwave oven on high and bake for 10 minutes. Let the mix cool for 48 hours, stirring occasionally to aerate the mix. Baking the soil produces an unpleasant odor—so beware.

The disadvantage of garden soils of any sort is a lack of consistency in their quality: You simply never know what you are getting or how it will react when compacted into a pot.

Peat moss　Made up of various types of partially decomposed bog plants, peat moss is the basic element of most modern potting mixes, even soil-based ones. It adds lightness to a mix and improves water retention. Since it expands when moist and contracts when dry, it literally pulls air into the soil. Its main disadvantages are its tendencies to compact with time and become increasingly acidic. It contains almost no nutrients. The most popular type for potting mixes is Canadian sphagnum peat.

Vermiculite　This material is expanded mica, which looks like little flakes of gold. It has excellent aeration properties, and can absorb several times its weight in water and minerals, and releases them slowly. Its main disadvantage is a tendency to become compact with time. The fine and medium grades are most popular. Use only horticultural vermiculite; construction-grade vermiculite sometimes contains harmful impurities.

Perlite　This white expanded volcanic rock helps maintain good aeration in a mix. Like vermiculite, it absorbs excess minerals and water, releasing them over time. Unlike vermiculite, it does not compact significantly with time, making it a choice ingredient for a potting mix for mature plants. Coarse to medium grades are preferable. Perlite tends to rise to the surface when the plant is watered.

Charcoal　Although it is often absent from commercial mixes, charcoal is worth adding even if you don't mix your own soil. It acts as a buffer in the potting mix, absorbing potentially harmful excess minerals as well as toxins resulting from decomposition. Use only horticultural- or aquarium-grade charcoal, and sift it first to remove the dust. Never add barbecue charcoal to a potting mix.

Sphagnum moss　This bog moss is used for plants such as epiphytes, or air plants, that require a very airy yet humid growing medium. Long-strand sphagnum moss is sometimes sold in living (still green) form, but you're more likely to find it dried and golden brown. Before using, soak it in warm water, and use it only with some form of lime to counteract its high acidity. A milled form is often used in seed mixtures to help prevent damping-off, a fungus resembling mildew, but is too fine for use in regular potting mixes. New Zealand sphagnum moss is increasingly popular.

Bark　Fine grades of ground tree bark are sometimes substituted for peat moss. Coarser grades are commonly found in epiphytic mixes used for orchids and bromeliads because they provide excellent aeration.

Calcined clay　Composed of chunks of kiln-hardened clay, calcined clay is most widely available in the form of unscented cat litter. It adds aeration and drainage to a mix and absorbs excess water. It makes a good substitute for both vermiculite and perlite when a heavier mix is desired. Always sift it to remove the dust before adding it to a mix.

Coarse sand　Used mainly in succulent mixes, coarse sand adds weight to a potting mix and improves drainage. Use only horticultural or washed sand.

Choosing the right potting mix for each species helps ensure that all of your houseplants will thrive.

Dolomitic lime   A white powder, dolomitic lime is added in small quantities to mixes, especially peat-based ones, to reduce their acidity.

Basic Soilless Mix

A good all-purpose potting mix is well suited to most indoor plants. A basic soilless mix can be made by combining 1 quart peat moss, 1 quart medium-grade vermiculite, 1 quart medium-grade perlite, 3 tablespoons dolomitic lime, and 1 cup sifted horticultural charcoal.

Basic Soil-Based Mix

This heavier mix is especially useful for plants that you don't want to repot annually. Mix together equal parts pasteurized garden loam and basic soilless mix or commercial soilless mix.

Bromeliads, such as those lining the floor of this sunroom, benefit from a potting mix that is airy and humid.

African Violet Mix

African violets, begonias, philodendrons, and azaleas grow well in a mixture that has a high humus content and is somewhat acidic. For these plants try equal parts sand, peat moss, pasteurized garden loam, and leaf mold. This type of soil premixed is sold as African violet mix.

Epiphytic Mix

Orchids, bromeliads, and other air plants, or epiphytes will do well in a mix of 1 quart longstrand or New Zealand sphagnum moss, 1 quart coarse bark, 1 quart coarse-grade perlite, 1 tablespoon dolomitic lime, and 1 cup sifted horticultural charcoal.

Cactus Mix

Plants from the desert need a growing medium that is gritty, neutral in pH, and low in organic matter. Most cacti and other succulents will prosper in a mixture of 2 quarts pasteurized garden loam, 1 quart coarse sand, 1 quart calcined clay, 2 tablespoons dolomitic lime, and ⅓ cup sifted horticultural charcoal.

Take advantage of soil amendments, even if you are using a commercially prepared mix. Horticultural perlite makes a good substitute for sand. Vermiculite, used in place of leaf mold, lightens and conditions heavy, sticky soil and makes it acceptable to plants that need a well-aerated medium.

POTS AND CONTAINERS

The particular pots you choose to grow your plants in directly influence how well they grow, what kind of care you should give them, and how good they look once planted.

Clay pots The standard clay pot is hard to beat because it is both functional and attractive. There are many shapes, but sizes generally range from 2 to 18 inches in diameter. Clay pots have a drainage hole in the bottom. Usually you can buy saucers to match.

Take precautions against the moisture that seeps through the bottom of clay saucers and can damage floors. A round of ½-inch-thick cork cut to fit beneath the saucer will dissipate the water. Plastic and glazed ceramic saucers are moisture-proof.

A blue-and-white glazed pot shows off these white tulips (Tulipa) to perfection.

Plastic pots   Being lightweight is the distinct advantage of plastic pots. They are generally less expensive than clay and come in the same range of sizes. In addition, they are not porous, as are clay pots, and therefore retain water much longer. They generally have several drainage holes. Plants in plastic containers do not need to be watered as often as those in clay pots. Because air does not move through the walls of these pots, drainage must be excellent.

Before you reuse clay and plastic pots, scrub them clean with a stiff brush and warm water. You can also sanitize them by soaking them in a 1:10 solution of household bleach and water.

Pottery containers   Glazed pottery containers can be highly decorative, especially for indoor plants. Many nurseries and garden centers now stock an array of sizes and designs in pottery containers, including pots and trays for bonsai that can also be used for other plants or for miniature landscapes.

If you select a container that does not have drainage holes, the best practice is to grow the plant in a slightly smaller clay or plastic pot that does, and simply slip this inside the more decorative container (see the section on cachepots and jardinieres below).

Woven baskets   Although woven baskets make attractive holders for plants, they rot quickly if subjected to constant moisture. Some baskets come lined with plastic, to prevent moisture from reaching the basket.

Planting directly in unlined baskets is unwise. It is better to use them purely for show, hiding a more utilitarian pot. Be sure to include a saucer inside the basket to collect water.

Hanging planters   These aerialists of the plant world allow you to get the most from the indoor gardening space you have. Hanging containers are at their best dangling or climbing—from beams, windows, above kitchen sinks, in corners, from skylights, or down stairwells.

You can use pottery, wood, wire, or plastic hanging planters, commonly available at stores, or adapt regular clay and plastic flowerpots to the purpose. You can buy all kinds of decorative hangers—twine, string, leather, wire, or chain—or you can make your own from materials found in hobby shops. Hangers can also hold a saucer in place to prevent water from dripping onto the floor.

It's a good idea to line wood planters with thick plastic or aluminum foil so that the potting mix won't wash through the cracks. Wire baskets (and plastic baskets with spaces between the ribs) need to be lined with coarse, unmilled sphagnum moss or sheet moss before you fill them with potting mix.

Even so, set these only above a masonry floor, such as you would find in a greenhouse or solarium, because they will still drip water. Some growers go one step further and include an additional lining of burlap or a saucer to prevent the potting mix from dripping.

Self-Watering Containers

The advantage of self-watering containers is a water reservoir that needs attention only when it gets low, usually every couple of weeks. Since fertilizer is usually added to the water at the same time, feeding and watering become chores to do every few weeks instead of every few days. Meanwhile, the pot automatically delivers water at the rate the plant uses it, adapting to changes

Baskets are ideal companions to plants; here an orchid adds a note of color to a basket collection.

in light, humidity, or temperature. Plants in self-watering containers are usually more evenly watered than plants growing in conventional pots. African violets (*Saintpaulia*) do especially well in self-watering containers.

There are many types of self-watering containers. Some have built-in reservoirs. Others are actually two pots: a grow pot and an outer pot that acts as a reservoir.

Although self-watering containers are essentially simple to operate, these few pointers will help you avoid any problems.

• Most wicks need to be primed (pre-moistened). Soak the wick in water before use. If the grow pot has a porous bottom designed to act as a wick, likewise let it soak in water for two hours before potting. After potting the plant, water it from the top the first time to prime that part of the system too.

• If the potting mix is constantly soggy, install a thinner wick. If it is always too dry, install a thicker wick or several wicks.

• Use only soilless mixes in self-watering containers. Garden soil tends to compact quickly when kept constantly moist.

• Never put a drainage layer of gravel or pot shards in the bottom of a self-watering container; it will stall the capillary action.

• Each time you top off the reservoir of a self-watering container, fertilize with a solution recommended for self-watering containers or a solution of water and soluble fertilizer diluted to one quarter the recommended strength.

• Leach the potting mix three or four times a year to remove accumulated fertilizer salts. Remove the reservoir and run tepid water through the grow pot until the drainage water runs perfectly clear.

• If your system works well for a while, then the potting mix suddenly remains dry no matter how much water is in the reservoir, it is time to change the wick.

Cachepots and Jardinieres

Although the pot the plant is growing in is often perfect for the cultural needs of the plant, it may not fit into the decorating scheme of a room. Then it's time to simply set the pot inside a decorative container, often called a cachepot or jardiniere.

Since the grow pot provides drainage for the plant, the outside container need not. Make sure that the container is at least 2 inches

Top: This light-filled bath is an ideal environment for these houseplants. Variegated ivy (Hedera helix) *and columnea trail downward and a dwarf anthurium* (Anthurium scherzeranum) *and maidenhair fern* (Adiantum) *find a home around the tub. Bottom: Self-watering containers come in a variety of sizes and styles.*

higher than the grow pot. Put a 1-inch layer of loose material that will not decompose, such as styrofoam chips and crushed chicken wire, in the bottom of the decorative container. Set the grow pot in the decorative pot and pack more of the bottom fill material around the sides. To hide the grow pot, spread a mulch composed of sphagnum moss, Spanish moss, bark chips, or water-polished stones over the surface.

Soak the grow pot thoroughly at each watering. The water that drains through to the decorative pot should evaporate. If it doesn't, loosen the top mulch to allow more air into the fill material.

Day-To-Day Care

Learning to take care of the everyday needs of your houseplants will help you ensure that they remain healthy and good-looking.

Houseplants are container plants, and the single most important concept to remember about container gardening is this: The roots of the plant are confined to the container; they cannot search deeper or wider for sustenance; therefore, the plant depends totally on you for nourishment and care.

The basic techniques for watering, fertilizing, and grooming can easily be applied to any plant. In the pages that follow, you'll find discussions of watering methods; fertilizers; and grooming, staking, and repotting techniques.

You'll also learn how to care for plants during their rest period and the steps to take for giving your indoor plants a vacation outdoors. Finally, you'll learn about the common pests and problems that can beset plants, as well as the treatments for each.

Most of the plants described in the "Gallery of Houseplants," beginning on page 69, will thrive with the standard culture techniques discussed in this chapter. Unusual requirements are spelled out where appropriate.

With a few simple tools and the knowledge of what your plants need, you will easily be able to keep your plants healthy.

Lack of water will quickly cause your plants to wilt and die.

HOW AND WHEN TO WATER

Improper watering is a major reason that houseplants die, and overwatering is the culprit more often than underwatering. Too much water coupled with poor drainage forces plant roots to sit in water, suffocate, and rot. When roots are unable to carry enough necessary oxygen to the rest of the plant, the result is wilt and decline. To avoid this problem don't assume immediately that your plant needs water when it doesn't grow as you had expected. Your good intentions will be harmful if the plant is suffering from some other ailment.

Water needs are related to several factors. Individual species have specific preferences dictated long ago in their natural habitats. The overall light, temperature, and humidity levels you provide for your plants will further affect and change moisture needs.

How much moisture a plant uses also depends on the size and type of container it grows in; if the pot is small, moisture will be absorbed quickly and the plant will have to be watered often. If you can't keep a plant moist, even if you water every day, then it needs a larger pot.

Water needs are also determined by the plant's growth cycle. During active growth periods a plant will absorb more water than during its rest periods.

Your job is to learn exactly when your plant needs water. The simplest and most reliable way to tell is to insert your finger into the potting mix and test by touch; you'll be able to feel the degree of moisture. To double-check, rub a bit of the mix between your thumb and index finger. With a little experience you'll be able to tell into which of the following three general moisture categories your potting mix fits at any given time.

Evenly moist: The potting mix is moist throughout but not so wet as to be soggy. The mix just below the surface will get your finger damp but not muddy. Ferns, gardenias, and African violets (*Saintpaulia*) grow well at this moisture level.

Slightly damp: The potting mix is dry on the surface, with low moisture just below the surface. The mix is cool and damp to the touch but won't get your finger wet. Coleus, monstera, and philodendrons are among the plants that prefer this level.

Moderately dry: The potting mix feels dry to the touch. It is dry below the surface to a depth of an inch; any deeper and it's time to water. Peperomia, dieffenbachia, dracaena, and geraniums (*Pelargonium*) thrive at this moisture level.

When you've determined the moisture level of a plant's potting mix, you can compare it with the optimum level for the plant recommended in the "Gallery of Houseplants," starting on page 69.

Always water thoroughly. If your plant doesn't receive thorough soakings but only superficial waterings, its roots will grow toward the surface of the potting mix. Every plant needs a thorough soaking; it's the frequency of watering that varies.

Water each plant until the potting mix is saturated. The water should take a minute or two to drain. If it doesn't drain after 10 to 15 minutes, check to be sure that the drainage

Top left: Most plants are watered from above. Be sure that there is a saucer to catch the runoff.
Top right: Once the water has drained, pour off any excess. Do not let water sit in the saucer.
Bottom left: You can water plants from below by filling the saucer with water. Fuzzy-leaved plants, such as African violets (Saintpaulia), prefer this method.
Bottom right: If a plant is too heavy to lift, draw off excess water with a turkey baster.

hole is not blocked. If it drains through very rapidly, it may be just running down between the rootball and the pot and not soaking into all of the rootball.

Watering in the morning allows any moisture on the foliage to evaporate by evening. Foliage that remains cool and wet is more prone to disease.

Never let plants sit in water. If the pot is in a saucer, pour off any drained water within an hour. If the plant is too heavy to lift, use a turkey baster to remove the water.

Water temperature is important. Tropical plants are the most sensitive, but all plants can be harmed by having cold or hot water applied either to the roots or to the foliage. Always use tepid water.

Water softeners that replace the calcium in water with sodium produce water that will harm plants. Sodium accumulates in the potting mix and does not settle out or evaporate. If you have a water softener, use a tap that is outdoors or install a tap in the water line before it goes into the softener so you'll have a source of unsoftened water for plants.

In parts of the country where the soil is very alkaline and the water is very hard (containing a heavy concentration of minerals), it is diffi-

cult to grow acid-loving plants such as azaleas. Adding peat moss or other acidic soil amendments to the potting mix and using fertilizers that have an acid reaction will help.

In alkaline conditions plants cannot use trace minerals and iron. They will therefore benefit from regular applications of an iron chelate, available at nurseries and garden centers, to keep the foliage a healthy green color. When the new foliage on these plants is yellow, water with a solution of 1 ounce iron sulfate in 2 gallons water. Repeat this every two weeks until growth regains a normal color.

If a plant is wilting or drooping and if the potting mix has completely dried out, the plant is thirsty—it needs water at once! Water a plant in this condition and try not to let this happen often. A plant that wilts again and again will not survive long.

There are times when your plants need more water than a shower from a watering can. The following techniques are useful for these occasions.

Watering from the bottom Many people find that watering plants from the bottom is easier and faster than top watering. Pour water into the saucer. Capillary action will cause the water to seep up and moisten the entire rootball. Make sure that the saucers you have

A plant that is wilting needs water immediately.

Left: Submerge a plant that is wilting in water up to the rim of the pot. Let the plant sit until no more air bubbles rise.
Right: Once most wilting plants have been given water, they will revive. Try not to let your plants get in this condition often.

Sturdy Houseplants

If plant after plant has faded away on you, don't give up on growing houseplants completely. You may simply have been trying the wrong plants! Many of the most commonly available plants, such as chrysanthemums, azaleas, cyclamens, and cinerarias, often given as gift plants, are, in fact, specifically grown for sale as temporary decorations: They were never intended to survive more than a few days to a few weeks. Other plants, such as camellias, gardenias, and jasmines, require continual care and optimal conditions to flourish. No wonder you haven't been able to keep them alive!

Fortunately, there are other houseplants that are inherently tough. They are able to withstand neglect for months or even years at a time and still look good. Many successful indoor gardeners got their start with them before moving on to the ones that do require some experience, so why not follow in their footsteps?

All the plants listed here will survive long periods without water, tolerate everything from low light to very intense light, and can even withstand dry indoor air. About the only thing they will not survive are temperatures below freezing.

Probably the toughest plant of all is the snakeplant (*Sansevieria*). It seems to thrive on neglect, growing slowly but surely no matter what the conditions. Its straight up-and-down, sculptural look suits many indoor decors.

Second place would probably go to the cast-iron plant (*Aspidistra elatior*), which lives up to its common name. Its growth in most indoor conditions is almost nil, but at least it survives.

The Chinese evergreen (*Aglaonema commutatum*) is another good choice. Its dense, arching growth and leathery leaves, often feathered with silver, seem to be able to take just about any kind of abuse. It is closely related to the peace-lily (*Spathiphyllum*), another tough plant that will occasionally produce a beautiful white flower, despite your lack of efforts.

The toughest of the hanging and climbing plants is that old staple, the heart-leaf philodendron (*Philodendron scandens*). Its two close relatives, the arrowhead vine (*Syngonium podophyllum*) and the pothos (*Epipremnum aureum*), are just about as resilient. The jade plant (*Crassula argentea*) prefers bright light to full sun, but it also will survive in less-than-ideal conditions.

Other plants that are very tolerant of poor conditions include the bottle palm (*Beaucarnea*), dieffenbachias, dracaenas, and a few palms (*Chamaedorea elegans* and *Rhapis excelsa*).

However, even tough plants can have a hard time if you don't choose correctly in the first place. Avoid young plants in small pots, for example; they require more care than established plants. Also, young plants don't grow very fast—and tough generally means slow; they may take years to reach the size you want. Never buy bargain plants either. They usually have not been acclimated to indoor growing conditions and will likely go downhill quickly. Instead, be prepared to pay a bit more to buy a plant from a specialized nursery that guarantees its product.

---

each plant in will hold enough water to saturate the potting mix. After about an hour, drain off any excess water that is left in the saucer.

Plants that are watered from below must be leached or flushed out at least once every few months to wash out mineral salts that can build up in the potting mix. To do this, water the plant copiously from above, let it drain, then repeat the process two or three more times. This is most easily done in a sink, a bathtub, or outdoors.

Submerging It is easier and faster to water container plants from above, but submerging a pot in water up to its rim is excellent for plants you've allowed to dry out completely and for those that are in full bloom. Leave the pot submerged for several minutes after the air stops bubbling up. This is always the best way to

water hanging plants or plants such as epiphytes, or air plants, which are often grown on pieces of bark. Drain the plant thoroughly before returning it to its growing space.

Showering An occasional rinse in the shower is an effective way to water plants thoroughly and to remove dust and dirt from the leaves. Use tepid water, with a gentle flow so that the potting mix does not wash out of the container. To avoid burning the leaves, make sure that they're dry before returning the plant to direct sunlight.

Leaching Thorough watering will also help wash out accumulated fertilizer salts, which can build up and harm the plant. This buildup can be caused by overfertilizing and by watering too little to drain the salts. It is recognizable by a whitish deposit on the outside of clay pots or by salt burn on the edges of leaves. Place the plant in a sink, tub, or pail and water it several times, each time letting the water drain. If salts have become a problem, they will not leach out in one day; the process may have to be repeated weekly for several weeks. Another remedy is to repot the plant into a new container.

HOW AND WHEN TO FERTILIZE

Fertilizers provide the nutritive minerals that plants require for healthy growth. Plants that need to be fertilized exhibit slow growth, pale leaves, weak stems, small or nonexistent flowers, or dropped leaves.

Nitrogen, phosphorus, and potassium are the three major nutrients needed by plants. When you pick up a container of houseplant fertilizer at your garden store, you'll see three numbers on the label. These are, in order, the percentages of nitrogen, phosphorus, and potassium. For example, a fertilizer labeled 12-6-6 is made up of 12 percent nitrogen, 6 percent phosphate, and 6 percent potash.

Fertilizers come in many different formulations. Those designed for flowering plants usually contain less nitrogen because nitrogen encourages foliage and stem growth and a deep green color, but at some expense of flowering. Phosphorus encourages bloom and root growth. Potassium contributes to stem strength and disease resistance.

In addition to these primary nutrients, plants need three secondary nutrients—sulfur, calcium,

Fertilizer tabs inserted into the potting mix release needed nutrients.

and magnesium. Plants also require minute quantities of iron, zinc, manganese, copper, chlorine, boron, and molybdenum. The latter are called micronutrients, or trace minerals.

As well as being manufactured in many formulations, fertilizers are available in many forms: water-soluble pellets, powders, liquids, dry tablets and sticks to insert in the potting mix, and time-release pellets. The variety can be confusing, and value does vary widely. Any reliable nurseryperson will help you choose the best fertilizer for your needs.

When applying fertilizers, always read the label first and follow the directions carefully. Don't succumb to the notion that more is better. It takes only a little extra fertilizer to burn a plant's roots or leaves.

Many houseplant fertilizers on the market have been formulated for use every two weeks. This is more effective and safer than large monthly doses. If monthly doses are recommended, you can feed half the suggested amount every two weeks.

Container plants need regular feeding only when they are in active growth. Dormant or sick plants never benefit from the addition of fertilizer. Dormant plants are in a natural state of arrested growth and fertilizer is not needed. Wilting, yellowing, pallid plants that are suffering from something other than lack of fertilizer will decline even more rapidly if you feed them. These plants are in a state of shock and may even die if fed.

Before turning to fertilizers, review the care requirements of the plant and determine whether you have been meeting them properly. If you have been fertilizing regularly and the plant isn't growing, it's likely that the plant is dormant or sick.

Too much fertilizer causes leaf tips and edges to turn brown in otherwise good growing conditions. Excess fertilizer also can cause premature dropping of the lower leaves and wilting of the entire plant. If you overfeed a plant, leach out the fertilizer by applying copious amounts of water. Allow the potting mix to drain, then pour on more water. As a last resort, you can wash the old mix from the roots and repot into fresh new mix.

Constant feeding One of the most recommended methods of fertilizing is using a constant-feed program; in other words, plants are fertilized lightly each time they are watered. Many plants, including African violets (*Saintpaulia*), can be fertilized this way every time they are watered, the year around. Other plants should be fed lightly with each watering only while they are actively growing and flowering.

When plants are fertilized constantly, growth is more symmetrical and leaf color and size are also more even. However, you must use a fertilizer formulated especially for this purpose. If you do not, you risk overfertilizing and damaging the roots.

Foliar feeding In their native habitats, plants can absorb nitrogen and other nutrients from rain and bird droppings that fall onto their leaves. You can duplicate this effect with fertilizers recommended for foliar application, available at garden stores. Apply these with a sprayer or mister every two to four weeks, following the label directions. Indoor gardeners often apply trace elements as foliar sprays. Foliar feeding is quick acting, lasts a relatively short time, and is best used as a supplement to a fertilizer applied directly to the potting mix.

GOOD GROOMING TECHNIQUES

Plants in containers need grooming to keep them manageable in size and attractive in shape. Good grooming also reduces the possibility of disease and helps flowering plants produce better blossoms. There are several methods for keeping plants in good shape.

Cleaning Dust and dirt on leaves keep light from reaching the leaf pores. Cleaning the plant allows the leaves to breath, and also helps rid them of insect eggs and mites.

For smooth-leaved plants, dampen a clean cloth or soft sponge in mild soapy water. Support the leaf in one hand while gently wiping away from the stem. Avoid cleaning new growth. These plants may also benefit from an occasional shower (see page 31).

Use a clean, dry, soft hairbrush or paintbrush to clean the fuzzy leaves of plants such as African violet (*Saintpaulia*) and velvetplant (*Gynura aurantiaca*). For large plants with many tiny leaves, such as weeping fig (*Ficus benjamina*), a feather duster—especially one made with ostrich feathers—is ideal for cleaning.

Always be careful in cleaning your houseplants not to spread pests or diseases from an infested plant to others. Disinfect cleaning materials with a 1:10 solution of household bleach and water and let dry. You can also spray cleaning materials with a disinfectant after use. Let them air out for a day or so after disinfecting them, to avoid any damage to the plant.

Trimming Once a leaf has turned entirely yellow, it will never become green again. Remove it to improve both the look of the plant and its general health. For the same reasons, a tip of a leaf that turns yellow or brown should be trimmed away. When cutting, use sharp shears and follow the original shape of the leaf, taking as little vital green material as possible. Small discolored leaves should be pinched off at the base of their stems.

Yellow and brown leaves are not always signs that a plant is ailing. Some attrition is part of the natural growth cycle of most plants.

Top: Trim any sections of leaves that have turned yellow. Follow the original shape of the leaf and take as little vital green material as possible. Bottom: Pinching a plant forces it to branch out and become bushier.

Pinching Using your thumb and forefinger to remove the young tip growth of a stem is called pinching the plant. This simple operation forces the plant to branch out below the pinch and become fuller and bushier.

Pinching works well for virtually all plants, but especially for soft-stemmed plants such as wax begonias (*Begonia* × *semperflorens*), angel-wing begonias, young geraniums (*Pelargonium*), and coleus (*Coleus* × *hybridus*).

Pruning To shape a plant attractively and invigorate it, pruning may be called for. Pruning refers to removing young woody stems. If a stem is removed at its point of origin, the result will be opening up space within the stem framework. New growth will take place in the stems remaining or from the base of the plant. If the stem is cut off above a leaf, one or more new growth tips will grow near the pruned tip to make the plant denser.

To prune properly, you will need a good pair of small hand pruners. With timely pruning, plants such as miniature rose, fuchsia, gardenia, and flowering maple will blossom more profusely, and the branch framework will be well balanced and sturdy. After a flowering period, clip off the spent blooms and long, weak branches that extend beyond the plant's overall shape.

PLANT SUPPORTS

Stakes, trellises, and other means of support are necessary for certain houseplants. These ensure healthy, attractive growth for climbing or vining plants such as bougainvillea, monstera, and philodendrons.

To train plants and to protect their fragile or elongated stems from breaking, staking is useful. Often, early in the life of a plant such as chrysanthemum, tuberous begonia (*Begonia* × *tuberhybrida*), or poinsettia (*Euphorbia pulcherrima*), each stem is tied to a stake (usually of dark green bamboo or wood). Moss sticks, available at garden centers and nurseries, are also commonly used to support many "climbing" philodendrons and other climbing plants.

Important points to remember are to stake early (you can keep a straight stem straight, but you may not be able to uncrook a crooked one) and to use pieces of soft yarn, strips of cloth, or the commercial wire twist-ties to tie the stems so that you don't injure them.

Although they are not seen frequently, trellises have a definite place in houseplant gardening. Vines grown on a trellis flourish whereas those that trail or hang grow more slowly because they lack the support they depend on. You can put up a small wood, wire, or string trellis wherever you want a vine to climb. In a sunny window, 'Heavenly Blue' morning glories or ivy geraniums make a cheerful drapery of flowers and foliage.

POTTING TECHNIQUES

Plants need repotting when they become pot bound—that is, when they grow too many roots for their containers. Tall plants, such as ficus, avocado (*Persea americana*), and certain dracaenas, need repotting when they start to look overgrown; they may topple if they become top-heavy. You can also repot plants into a handsome new container just to show off the plant.

In time, the roots of a plant gradually absorb all the minerals from the potting mix and form a tightly packed mass that inhibits growth. Repotting is essential at this time. A telltale sign is when a plant seems to need enormous amounts of water. To see if the roots are compacted, turn the plant on its side and knock the rim of the pot gently against a solid surface to loosen the rootball. If the roots are massed along the sides of the pot and at the base of the rootball, repot the plant.

In most instances it's advisable to repot a plant in a pot not more than 2 inches wider at the rim than the old pot. A pot that is much larger gives the roots a large space to grow into.

Left: Supporting a plant with stakes or a trellis lets you train it into a desired shape. Opposite top: Remove a plant from its existing pot by turning it on its side and knocking the rim of the pot gently against a solid surface. Opposite center: Place the plant in its new container and fill the container with potting mix. Opposite bottom: Gently tamp the new potting mix in place, then water thoroughly.

The top of the plant will not start to grow well until the roots begin to fill the container. Also, overpotting a plant can lead to root rot.

A good general rule about pot size is to use a pot whose diameter at the top of the rim equals one third to one half the height or, in the case of spreading plants, the diameter of the plant. However, very tall, slender plants will grow well in smaller pots.

If you are repotting a plant, be sure to use the same basic type of mix as before. If you wish to change types of mixes, you will need to gently wash all of the old mix off the plant roots before repotting.

Wet the potting mix before using it. About an hour before repotting, water the plant thoroughly. If you are potting into a new clay pot, soak the pot thoroughly (until air bubbles no longer rise from it) to ensure that it will not absorb water from the potting mix.

To remove the plant from its existing container, turn it on its side and knock the rim of the pot gently against a solid surface to loosen it. If the plant doesn't come out, the mix may be too wet. Let it dry a little, then try again. You can also run a sharp knife or spatula around the edge of the pot. Pull the plant out; you may need a second pair of hands to steady the pot.

If roots have circled around the inside of the container, prune them before transplanting. Make three or four ½-inch-deep cuts from the top of the rootball to the bottom with a sharp knife. The pruning will stimulate new root growth and help the roots penetrate the new mix surrounding the rootball.

To transplant, partly fill the new container with potting mix. Place the plant at the height it grew in its previous pot. Firm the potting mix around the rootball, then fill the container with additional mix.

Tamp the potting mix with your fingers, especially near the edges of the container. Water thoroughly and keep the roots moist until they have spread into the surrounding mix. Repot a plant as quickly as possible.

Occasionally a plant will need additional nourishment rather than repotting, especially if it performs better when pot bound. Such plants will benefit from a top dressing. To top-dress a plant, scrape off the top 1 to 2 inches of potting mix with a fork or small rake. Then fill the pot to its original level with fresh potting mix, tamping it firmly in place.

Pests and Problems

I nspect your plants each time you water to spot any problems, pests, and diseases before they do extensive damage. Use this chart to solve any problems that occur. Insects are usually brought indoors on new plants. Check new plants carefully before placing them in your home, and isolate any plants, new or old, with pests or diseases. If you need to use a pesticide or an insecticide, take care to follow the directions precisely and always check the label to be sure that the remedy is suitable for the plant and the problem you are treating. Apply pesticides formulated for indoor use. If you use a recommended pesticide that is not strictly for indoor use, be sure to take your infested plant outdoors and spray in a shady area.

CULTURAL PROBLEMS

Lack of Light	**Problem:** New growth is weak and spindly with large gaps between the leaves. Flowering plants fail to produce flowers, and plants with colorful foliage become pale. If most of the available light is coming from one direction, plants bend their stems and leaves in that direction. **Solution:** Gradually move the plant to a brighter location. Most plants will tolerate some direct sun if they are kept well watered. If a brighter location is not available, provide artificial light as described on pages 13 to 15.
Nitrogen Deficiency	**Problem:** The oldest leaves—usually the lower ones—turn yellow and may drop. Yellowing starts at the leaf margins and progresses inward without producing a distinct pattern and may progress upward until only the newest leaves remain green. Growth is slow, new leaves are small, and the whole plant may be stunted. **Solution:** For a quick response, spray the leaves with a foliar fertilizer. Fertilize houseplants with a soluble, nitrogen-rich plant food. Add the fertilizer at regular intervals, as recommended on the label.
Salt Damage	**Problem:** The leaf margins of plants with broad leaves or the leaf tips of plants with long, narrow leaves turn brown and die. This browning occurs on the older leaves first, but when the condition is severe, new leaves may also be affected. On some plants, the older leaves may turn yellow and die. **Solution:** Leach excess salts from the potting mix by flushing with water (see page 31). Never let a plant stand in drainage water. Trim off dead leaf tips.
Sunburn or Bleaching	**Problem:** Dead tan or brown patches develop on leaves that are exposed to direct sunlight. Or leaf tissue may lighten or turn gray. In some cases, the plant remains green, but growth is stunted. Damage is most severe when the plant is allowed to dry out. **Solution:** Move plants that cannot tolerate direct sun to a shaded spot. Or cut down the light intensity by closing the curtains when direct sun shines on the plant. Prune off badly damaged leaves or trim away damaged leaf areas to improve the plant's appearance. Keep plants properly watered.
Too Little Water	**Problem:** Leaves are small, and plant fails to grow well. Growth may be stunted. Plant parts or the whole plant may wilt. Margins of leaves or tips of leaves of narrow-leaved plants may dry and become brittle but still retain a dull green color. Bleached areas may occur between the veins. Such tissues may die and remain bleached or turn tan or brown. Plant may die. **Solution:** Water plants immediately and thoroughly. If the potting mix is completely dry, add a drop of liquid soap to the water or soak the entire pot in water for a couple days. If a plant is so dried out that it appears dead, soaking it could lead to root rot. Instead, give it a little water, gradually increasing the amount over several weeks.
Too Much Water or Poor Drainage	**Problem:** Plants fail to grow and may be wilting. Leaves lose their glossiness and may become light green or yellow. An examination of the rootball reveals mushy brown roots without white tips. The potting mix in the bottom of the pot may be very wet and may have a foul odor. Plants may die. **Solution:** Discard severely wilted plants and those without white root tips. Do not water less severely affected plants until the potting mix is barely moist. Prevent the problem by using light mixes with good drainage.
Water Spots	**Problem:** Small, somewhat angular light tan to reddish brown spots appear on the upper surfaces of the leaves. These spots are scattered and are found most frequently on the older leaves. **Solution:** Avoid getting cold water on the leaves when watering. Tepid water will not spot the leaves. Spotted leaves will not recover; pick them off if they are unsightly. Keep plants with wet leaves out of direct sunlight or they will burn.

Lack of light

Sunburn or bleaching

Nitrogen deficiency

Salt damage

Too little water

Too much water or poor drainage

Water spots

Pests and Problems (continued)

DISEASES AND PESTS

Aphids	**Problem:** Leaves are curling, discolored, and reduced in size. A shiny or sticky substance may coat the leaves. Tiny, nonwinged, soft-bodied green insects cluster on the buds, young stems, and leaves. **Solution:** Place a sticky trap next to the plant. If the infestation is bad, apply a household insecticide containing acephate (Orthene®), resmethrin, malathion, or pyrethrins. Make sure that your plant is listed on the product label and follow label directions carefully.
Botrytis or Gray Mold	**Problem:** Brown spots and blotches appear on the leaves and possibly on the stems. Spots on flowers may be white, tan, brown, or purple. If stems are infected, they may rot, causing the top part of the plant to topple and die. Under humid conditions, the infected portions may be covered with a fuzzy gray or brown growth. **Solution:** Remove all diseased and dead plant material promptly, particularly old flowers. Treat the rest of the plant with a fungicide, such as chlorothalonil. Make sure that your plant is listed on the product label and follow label directions carefully. To prevent this disease, avoid splashing water on the foliage and flowers, and avoid growing plants under crowded conditions where air is damp and still. Provide good air circulation around plants, but protect them from cold drafts. If the problem persists, grow plants in a warmer spot.
Crown, Stem, and Root Rot	**Problem:** Plants fail to grow. Lower leaves turn yellow. Leaves in the plant's center turn dark green, then black. Roots are dead and rotted. Plant may wilt and die. **Solution:** If plant is only mildly affected, let the potting mix dry out between waterings. Transplant into fast-draining potting mix in a container that drains freely. Discard severely infested plants and clean and disinfect pots (see page 24).
Fungus Gnats	**Problem:** Small, slender, dark insects fly around when plants are disturbed. They frequently run across the foliage and soil, and may also be found on windows. Roots may be damaged, and seedlings may die. **Solution:** Place a sticky trap next to the plant. If the infestation is bad, apply a household insecticide containing diazinon. Repeated applications may be necessary. Keeping the potting mix drier helps eliminate fungus gnats.

Aphids

Crown, stem, and root rot

Botrytis or gray mold

Fungus gnats

Pests and Problems (continued)

DISEASES AND PESTS

Leafminers	**Problem:** Irregular, winding white tunnels or patches appear on upper leaf surfaces. Small, dark-headed white grubs may be seen in the tunnels. **Solution:** Remove infested leaves. If the infestation is bad, apply a household insecticide containing acephate (Orthene®). Make sure that your plant is listed on the product label and follow label directions carefully.
Leaf Spot	**Problem:** Round reddish-brown spots surrounded by a yellow margin appear on leaves. Badly spotted leaves may turn yellow and die. **Solution:** Clip off badly spotted leaves. Water carefully to avoid leaf splash, and keep the foliage dry to prevent the spread of *Fusarium moniliforme,* the fungus responsible. If the problem continues, apply a fungicide containing chlorothalonil. Make sure that your plant is listed on the product label and follow label directions carefully.
Mealybugs	**Problem:** Cottony or waxy white insects are on the undersides of the leaves, on the stems, and particularly in the crotches or where leaves are attached. Cottony masses that contain eggs of the insects may also be present. A sticky substance may cover the leaves or drop onto surfaces below the plant. Infested plants are unsightly, do not grow well, and may die if severely infested. **Solution:** Control of mealybugs is difficult. The waxy coverings on the insects and egg sacs and the tendency for the insects to group together protect them from insecticides. If only a few mealybugs are present, wipe them off with a damp cloth, or use cotton swabs dipped in rubbing alcohol. Carefully check all parts of the plant to make sure that all insects are removed. Wipe off any egg sacs under the rims or bottoms of pots. If the plant is more heavily infested, thoroughly apply a houseplant insecticide containing acephate (Orthene®) or resmethrin and oil to stems and both sides of leaves, or spray outdoors with a general-purpose pesticide containing malathion. Make sure that your plant is listed on the product label and follow label directions carefully. Discard severely infested plants. Inspect new plants before bringing them into the house.

Leafminers

Leaf spot

Mealybugs

Pests and Problems (continued)

DISEASES AND PESTS

Powdery Mildew	**Problem:** Powdery white or gray patches appear on leaves, stems, and flowers. It begins on the upper surface of older leaves. Tissue underneath may turn yellow or brown and affected leaves may drop. Powdery mildew is caused by fungi. **Solution:** Remove infected leaves and apply a fungicide, such as triforene or chlorothalonil, until disease is gone. Make sure that your plant is listed on the product label and follow label directions carefully. Move plant to a location with more light and more even air temperature, and provide better air circulation. Keep out of cool drafts.
Scale Insects	**Problem:** Nodes, stems, and leaves are covered with cottony, cushionlike white masses or crusty brown bumps or clusters of scaly, somewhat flattened reddish gray or brown bumps. The bumps can be scraped or picked off easily. Leaves turn yellow and may drop. A shiny or sticky material may cover the leaves. **Solution:** Pick off by hand, using a soft brush dipped in soapy water. If the problem is bad, apply a household insecticide containing acephate (Orthene®) or resmethrin and oil. Make sure that your plant is listed on the product label and follow label directions carefully. Spraying is most effective against the crawlers rather than against adults. Repeated applications may be necessary. Treatment is most efficient if visible scales are first removed by hand.
Sooty Mold	**Problem:** Patches of thin black powder appear on both surfaces of the leaf. Leaves yellow and die from lack of light. This is a side effect from an infestation of mealybugs, scale insects, or whiteflies. **Solution:** Remove yellowed leaves and rinse off healthy ones with soap and water. Treat plant for insect infestation.
Spider Mites	**Problem:** Leaves are stippled, yellowing, and dirty. Leaves may dry out and drop. There may be webbing over the flower buds, between leaves, or on the lower surface of the leaves. To determine whether a plant is infested with mites, hold a sheet of white paper underneath an affected leaf and tap the leaf sharply. Minute green, red, or yellow specks the size of pepper grains will drop to the paper and begin to crawl around. **Solution:** Apply a household insecticide containing hexakis (Vendex®), acephate (Orthene®), or resmethrin, or try an insecticidal soap. Make sure that your plant is listed on the product label and follow label directions carefully. Repeat weekly for several weeks to kill the mites as they hatch from the eggs. To avoid introducing mites into your house, inspect newly purchased plants carefully. Increasing humidity around the plant will also help prevent them.
Thrips	**Problem:** Flowers and leaves are mottled or streaked with silver. Dusty black droppings collect on leaves or flowers. Tiny insects scuttle away when the plant is breathed on. **Solution:** Remove heavily damaged leaves and flowers. Apply a household insecticide containing acephate (Orthene®) or resmethrin weekly until no further symptoms are apparent. Make sure that your plant is listed on the product label and follow label directions carefully.
Whiteflies	**Problem:** Tiny, winged insects feed mainly on the undersides of the leaves. The insects are covered with a waxy white powder. When the plant is touched, insects flutter around it. Leaves may be mottled and yellow. A sugary material may coat the leaves. **Solution:** Remove heavily infested leaves as soon as the problem is spotted. If only a few leaves are infested, wipe off larvae with a damp cloth or cotton swabs soaked in alcohol, or vacuum them up. Place a sticky trap next to the plant. If problem worsens, apply a houseplant insecticide containing acephate (Orthene®), resmethrin-petroleum oil spray, malathion, or pyrethrins, or try insecticidal soaps. Make sure that your plant is listed on the product label and follow label directions carefully.

Scale insects

Powdery mildew

Sooty mold

Thrips

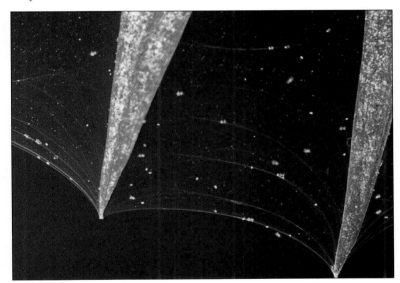

Spider mites

Whiteflies

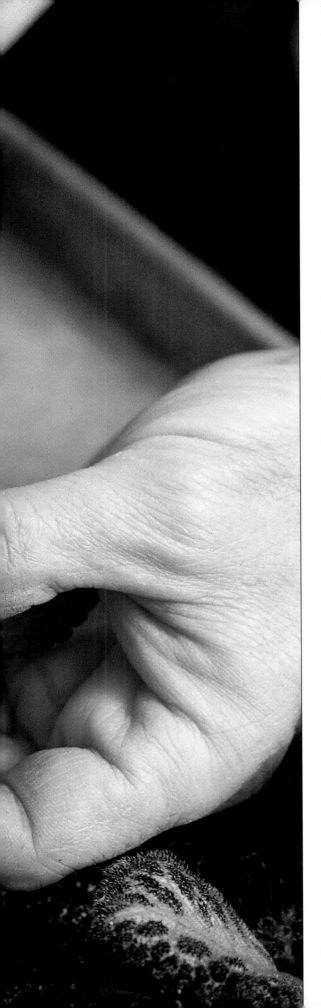

Propagation

Propagating new plants from existing ones, or growing a houseplant from seed, adds an entirely new dimension to your enjoyment of indoor gardening.

Propagation—the creation of new plants from old ones—is one of the most rewarding, easy, and economical ways to support your plant-growing habit. Besides saving you money, propagating your own plants gives you direct control over the quality of your plants as well as providing you with the enjoyable experience of being involved with them from their first days of growth.

Plants propagate in two fundamentally different ways—sexually and asexually. Sexual propagation occurs when the male and female parts of the plant unite to produce seeds. Asexual propagation, also known as vegetative propagation, occurs when a piece of a plant is cultivated and grown. The new plant is simply a young extension of the original parent plant.

There are a wide array of vegetative propagation techniques. The one you choose depends on the specific plant you wish to propagate and the method you prefer. The following discussion will help familiarize you with the various techniques for propagating plants and the types of plants suitable to each. You'll also discover how best to grow plants from seeds and ferns from spores.

Propagating plants lets you become intimately involved in a plant's growing process.

CUTTINGS

Taking a part of a plant and inducing it to form roots is the most popular method of vegetative propagation. Cut a piece of an existing plant, remove the lower leaves, plant the cutting in a rooting mix, and wait until roots form. Once several branched roots have formed, the cutting is ready to be planted in a pot.

This basic method varies, depending on the plant you root and the conditions in which you choose to propagate it. Most plants with soft stems, such as impatiens, are easy to propagate by this method. Others with woody stems, such as the older growth on camellias, are more difficult.

Top: Many plants can be propagated from a single leaf. Use a broken leaf or cut one off the parent plant. Bottom: Make a diagonal cut at the base of the stem with a sharp knife, then place the cutting in a moistened growing medium and cover it with plastic for a few days.

Depending on the plant, cuttings from some parts of the plant work better than others. Stem cuttings are the most familiar, but you can also root cuttings from leaves and pieces of root.

Stem cuttings   Use a sharp knife or razor blade to cut off a healthy piece of growth, usually 4 to 6 inches long. Cut at an angle just below a node—the joint from which both leaves and new roots normally arise. Trim the base with a clean cut about ⅛ inch above the lowest leaf node. There should be at least one node on the cutting.

Remove the lower two or three leaves and any flower buds or blossoms you find on your cutting. If the cutting has many leaves, remove enough that none will come into contact with the rooting mix; this can sometimes cause leaves to decay.

When taking a cutting from a plant with a milky sap, such as a fig (*Ficus*) or geranium (*Pelargonium*), make the cut and rub the cut end with denatured alcohol to prevent disease. Allow it to dry, or callus, for a few hours out of the sun, then plant it in the rooting mix.

Leaf cuttings   Some plants have the ability to propagate themselves from a single leaf cutting. Best known for this is the African violet (*Saintpaulia*), but the same technique works for rex begonias, florist's gloxinias (*Sinningia speciosa*), sedums, kalanchoes, and some peperomias.

Certain species produce new plants from only a section of a leaf, providing that the section contains a piece of the midrib. Cape primrose (*Streptocarpus*) can be propagated by laying leaf sections on top of the rooting mix. Leaf sections of the snakeplant (*Sansevieria trifasciata*) will root and grow if the base is inserted just below the surface of the rooting mix.

To start a new plant from a leaf cutting, pull or cut a mature, but not obviously old, leaf away from the parent plant. Cut the leaf stem to ½ to 1 inch in length. Set the leaf in the rooting mix at a 45-degree angle (it can be resting against the side of the container), taking care not to place the cut end too deep in the mix. Once plantlets form, cut away the parent leaf and transplant the new cuttings.

Root cuttings   Some plants can be propagated from latent buds in their roots, including the edible fig (*Ficus carica*) and the Hawaiian ti plant (*Cordyline terminalis*). To propagate a plant from a root cutting, set the root pieces vertically in the rooting mix. The ends that were closest to the crown should be at the top. When plantlets form, transplant them as you would other types of cuttings.

How to root cuttings Different gardeners use different rooting mixes for cuttings. In all cases it is important that the mix holds a lot of water and is light and porous, so that air can circulate through the material and reach the roots. One of the best rooting mixes is a mixture of 1 part sand and 1 part sphagnum peat moss. You also can use straight vermiculite, perlite, milled sphagnum moss, or 2 parts perlite to 1 part peat moss. Never use a soil-based mix as a rooting mix; it is subject to rot-causing pathogens. All rooting mixes should be sterilized before use.

Any number of containers can be used to root cuttings. Plastic pots are preferable to clay pots for cuttings because they retain moisture for a longer period of time. Plants such as columneas and begonias root so easily that you can place the cuttings directly in the final containers. Given reasonable humidity, a porous potting mix, and ample water, the cuttings will root within weeks and produce mature container plants in one season.

If you want to root a number of different cuttings, a clear plastic box or a plastic bag makes an excellent propagator. Use a heated ice pick to punch a few ventilation holes in the top. Add 2 inches of rooting mix to the bottom, moisten, then place your box in a bright, warm place out of direct sun. A sheet of polyethylene plastic or glass makes the "greenhouse" cover for the box. You can make a similar propagating box using a seed flat or fruit lug.

If you read your seed catalogs closely or read labels in garden center aisles, you may have noticed small containers of rooting hormone. It is available in both powder and liquid form. These products promote faster rooting and better root systems, especially in woody plants. You don't really need a rooting hormone for plants such as coleus or Swedish ivy (*Plectranthus*), which root quickly and easily; but plants with slightly woody stems—for example, fuchsia (*Fuchsia* × *hybrida*) and miniature rose (*Rosa*)—are much more apt to root if a hormone is used.

One method for rooting cuttings is to simply place them in a glass of water until roots form. Place each cutting in a separate glass and transplant when the roots are clearly visible but no longer than 1 inch. Water-rooted cuttings can be transplanted into a soilless mix (see page 21).

To root a cutting in a rooting mix, dust the cutting end with hormone powder, if you want. Then use your index finger or a pencil to make a hole in the rooting mix and insert the bare stem portion of the cutting. Firm the rooting mix around the cutting to hold it in place. Encase the entire cutting and container in a clear plastic bag. Use a stake or a loop of wire to

Top: Take a stem cutting from a herbacious plant, such as this geranium (Pelargonium) using a sharp knife. Bottom: Remove the lower leaves of the cutting as well as any excessive top growth.

Left: When planting a stem cutting, use a pencil to make a small hole in the rooting medium and insert the trimmed cutting into it.
Right: Cover the cutting with a plastic cup or a staked plastic bag. Remove the plastic cover after a few days.

support the plastic so that it does not touch the foliage. Finally, set the cutting in a bright, warm place. Do not place it in direct sunlight.

It is important to plant the cutting quickly after severing it from the mother plant. Often cuttings fail to root because they dry out before being planted.

You can tell when roots have begun to grow because the foliage will perk up and the new plant will put out new growth. Also, if you tug gently on the cutting, it will not pull out of the soil. Remove the plastic cover, at first for an hour or two daily, then for several hours. Finally, remove the cover and move the plant to its permanent growing place.

Be careful not to waterlog the rooting mix. Rooting boxes frequently don't have drainage holes, so overwatering will lead to root rot. If you are using a plastic bag or a plastic or glass cover, be sure to remove it for a few hours every day to allow fresh air to circulate.

The time needed for the rooting process varies from one to six weeks, depending on the plant. The best way to determine when it is ready to be transplanted is to check the roots. Gently lift the cutting out of the rooting mix

and observe the root length. The roots should not be much longer than an inch or they likely will tear off when you transplant the cutting.

It is important to move these new plants out of the sterile rooting mix and into a potting mix as soon as possible. There is some danger of nutrient deficiency and root rot if cuttings are left too long in the rooting mix.

DIVISION

This technique involves dividing one entire plant, including its root system and foliage, into two or more separate plants. Plants that have multiple basal stems are ideal candidates for division. This includes plants such as the cast-iron plant (*Aspidistra elatior*), most ferns, wax begonias (*Begonia* × *semperflorens*), most bromeliads, cluster-forming succulents such as certain sedums and crassulas, and African violets (*Saintpaulia*). When multiple stems have emerged from the base of a plant, you can divide it.

Foliage plants should be divided in early spring when the plants are just beginning to produce new growth. If your environmental conditions are moderately warm and humid, you can divide a plant at any time. Flowering plants are best divided during their dormant periods, when they are not flowering.

The easiest way to propagate by division is to slice down through the rootball with a sharp knife, severing the plant into two separate ones. Remember that you must get some of the main root and stem systems in each new division, or the plants cannot live.

Another way to divide a plant is to knock the entire plant out of its pot, rinse off the soil surrounding the roots, then gently break apart the plant by hand and replant each piece.

Plant the divisions immediately and water thoroughly to prevent the roots from drying out. Keep the divisions in bright light out of direct sun. Water the plants frequently until they root and appear upright and healthy. Then place them in their permanent location and resume normal care.

Offsets

Many plants, such as the screwpine (*Pandanus veitchii*), produce offsets, which are small plants that are still attached to the parent. They can be separated and planted in the same manner as division. Detach the offsets when they are mature enough to survive on their own.

Plantlets

Several common houseplants, such as the spiderplant (*Chlorophytum*) and many species of Boston fern (*Nephrolepis exaltata*), reproduce by sending out miniature plants on runners or shoots. When plantlets begin to form aerial roots, they can be separated from the parent.

Root the plantlets by filling a small pot with moist rooting mix and placing it alongside the parent plant. Without severing the runner, lay the plantlet on top of the rooting mix in the new pot and hold it in place with a hairpin or a piece of wire. Keep the rooting mix moist. New growth on the plantlet signals that it has rooted and can be separated from the parent plant.

Alternatively, clip off the runner and insert the base of the plantlet into moist rooting mix. Cover with glass or plastic film until the new roots form.

Unlike most other plants that propagate by stolons, the piggyback plant (*Tolmiea menziesii*) forms new plantlets on top of mature leaves. These are rooted in the same manner as other plantlets.

Top: To divide an offset from the parent plant, slice through the soil with a sharp knife, making sure that you take some of the basal growth and roots. Center: Pot the division in its own container and provide it with the same growing conditions as the parent plant. Bottom: Water the cup formed by the bromeliad leaves and very infrequently moisten the roots.

Plantlets formed on the runners or shoots of the spiderplant (Chlorophytum comosum) can be pinned into the moist potting mix in a pot and left to grow alongside the parent plant until they root.

Divide plants that grow from tubers by cutting the tuber into several pieces, making sure that each section has a bud. Dust each piece with fungicide and plant just below the surface of a moist rooting medium.

Tuber, Rhizome, Corm, and Bulb Division

Dividing tubers, rhizomes, corms, and bulbs is closely related to dividing plants with multiple basal stems. Tuber division works for large bulbs of florist's gloxinia (*Sinningia speciosa*), tuberous begonia (*Begonia* × *tuberhybrida*), and caladium. Simply cut the tuber as you would a seed potato, being sure that every part has a bud, or "eye." Dust the cut surface with fungicide, let it dry, and plant each piece in moist rooting mix. Provide good air circulation to reduce the chance of fungus or bacterial rot. Tuber division is best done just as the plants emerge from dormancy, not during their growing season.

The lovely glory lily (*Gloriosa rothschildiana*) produces cigar-shaped tubers, which can be broken into pieces and replanted. Ferns that form rhizomes can also be cut into pieces and replanted.

Theoretically, plants with corms, such as freesias, can be divided, but getting a bud in each division is tricky. It is easiest to replant many of the small new corms, called cormels, that form around the parent corm. Separate them and replant them about 2 inches deep.

Bulbs of the scaly type, such as Easter lilies (*Lilium longiflorum*), can be propagated by peeling off one or two layers of scales and laying the scales on the rooting mix. Dust the scales with fungicide and a rooting powder, and seal them in a plastic bag filled with damp vermiculite. Keep the bag at room temperature until bulblets form—about two months—and then cool them in the refrigerator for another two months before planting.

LAYERING

Propagating plants by layering them is similar to rooting cuttings, except that the part of the plant (usually a branch) that is to be rooted remains attached to the parent plant. The advantage of layering is that the parent plant supplies the cutting with water and nutrients while the roots are forming. Daily maintenance of the cuttings is therefore unnecessary.

To be suitable for layering, a plant needs to have a branch low enough so that you can bend it into contact with the potting mix. If there is such a branch, bend it, make a notch at the point of contact with the mix, then bury that portion of the branch. Securely immobilize it with a peg, a hairpin, a piece of light wire in the shape of a U, or a rock. A rock has the added advantage of keeping the soil beneath it moist.

Layering is best done in spring. Root formation is likely to take several months. Spring is also the best time for detaching the rooted branch, so you may want to leave the layer attached for a full year. When you are ready to detach the branch, lift it from the potting mix at the point where the roots have formed, then cut it from the parent plant and treat it as a rooted cutting.

A number of low-growing species, such as the screwpine (*Pandanus*), will self-layer. Detach the rooted branch and transplant it as you would a root cutting.

Air layering works well for plants such as dumb-cane (*Dieffenbachia*), dracaenas, rubber

plant (*Ficus elastica*), and pothos (*Epipremnum aureum*), which lack branches conveniently close to the ground for layering. It is especially useful for salvaging naturally leggy plants or mature specimens that have lost their lower leaves.

With a sharp knife, make a shallow cut no more than halfway through a stem at about a foot from the growing tip. Insert a thin piece of wood (such as a matchstick) to hold the cut open. Wrap the stem with a handful of coarse, wet sphagnum moss or a damp sponge, cover it with plastic wrap, and secure with tape or rubber bands above and below the cut. When new roots form in the moss, cut off the stem below the rooted section and pot the new plant.

If months go by before rooting occurs, you may have to wet the moss by poking a small hole in the wrap and squirting water inside. If

Top: To layer a plant, bend a low branch so that it is in contact with the potting mix. Notch the branch at the point of contact and bury it in the growing medium.
Bottom: Immobilize the rooting branch with a peg or rock and wait for it to root; it usually takes several months.

Top: To air-layer a plant, cut into, but not through, the stem with a sharp knife.
Center: Insert a wedge to keep the cut open, then cover the cut with damp moss and wrap it in plastic.
Bottom: When roots appear, cut off the stem and pot the rooted plant.

the stem fails to produce roots, try again: Open up the wrapping, nick the stem, dust the cut with rooting hormone, and retie.

GROWING PLANTS FROM SEED

A few houseplants such as asparagus ferns and primroses are easily raised from seed, but most require time, skill, and heated conditions for success—something most of us, unless we are professional horticulturists, do not have.

A seed is a tiny dormant plant waiting for the right conditions to begin its life cycle. To achieve this it must be given a disease-free growing medium, proper warmth and moisture, and adequate light for germination.

Seeds for houseplants are available from most quality seed sources. They may be sown by the same methods used for outdoor plants, with bottom heat (70° to 75° F) added to expedite germination. Bottom heat is a method of heating the planting area from below with electric coils. Inexpensive soil-heating cables are available in various sizes to meet your needs. A garden center will be able to supply the best type of unit for your use.

An easy way to start seeds is to sow them in moistened vermiculite or in milled sphagnum moss. Both are available at garden supply centers. Use flats, cartons, pots, or any container you desire. Small plastic "greenhouses"—trays with clear plastic covers—make excellent seed propagators.

Certain seeds must be treated before they will germinate. Some require stratification, or storage for six weeks or longer at a temperature of 35° to 40° F. Other seeds have a coat so tough that it must be broken before being planted. This treatment, called scarification, is achieved by nicking the seed coat with a file or sandpaper.

Sow seeds sparingly so that the seedlings don't get crowded and reduce the air circulation. Tiny dustlike seeds are scattered on top of the moist growing medium; leave them uncovered. Sow medium-sized seeds on the growing medium, then cover them with a thin layer of the medium to hold them in place when they are watered. Cover large seeds to a depth twice their diameter. Firm the vermiculite or sphagnum around the seeds by pressing gently.

Label each type of seed with name, date planted, and any other desired information.

Easy Plants to Propagate From Seed

Botanical Name	Common Name
Aglaonema modestum	Chinese evergreen
Asparagus species	Asparagus fern
Begonia × *semperflorens-cultorum*	Wax begonia
Bromeliad species	Bromeliad
Cacti species	Cactus
Coleus × *hybridus*	Coleus
Cyclamen persicum	Cyclamen
Exacum affine	Persian violet
Impatiens species	Impatiens
Peperomia species	Peperomia
Persea americana	Avocado
Saintpaulia species	African violet

Top: Growing ferns from spores takes time and patience, but the results are rewarding. Bottom: Plastic bags are useful miniature greenhouses for starting cuttings from seed.

Water lightly and slip the seed tray into a plastic bag or cover it with paper. Read the seed packets to see if light is required for germination. Follow the directions and check seeds daily, adding water if necessary.

When the seedlings emerge, move them to brighter light. The first two leaves to sprout are not true leaves but rather cotyledons, which nourish the stem tip and the foliage leaves (true leaves) that follow. Wait for the foliage leaves to appear before you place the seedlings in sunshine, then give them the same light you would the mature plant.

When the seedlings are three to five weeks old, fertilize every two weeks with a diluted liquid solution (one-quarter regular strength).

Transplant the seedlings when they have at least four true leaves. Dig them out carefully and place them into individual 2¼-inch pots filled with potting mix.

GROWING FERNS FROM SPORES

Unlike most plants, ferns produce dustlike spores, not seeds. It's a challenge to try to germinate these spores at home—they are tiny, very slow to germinate and grow, and must be protected continually from dry air.

Look for ripe spore cases on the underside of the fronds and brush the spores into an envelope. Allow them to dry for a few weeks before trying to germinate them.

One trick for germinating spores that is especially successful is the brick-and-box method.

Place a brick in a transparent plastic box. Add 2 inches of water. Cover the top of the brick with ¼ inch of milled peat moss. Sprinkle the spores on top of this layer of moss and cover the box with glass or plastic to retain moisture.

Place the box in a dimly lit spot with a moderate temperature (65° to 75° F) for several months. Add water to keep it at the 2-inch level. A mosslike growth will eventually appear on the top of the covered brick. This is the sexual stage of the fern. At this stage, transplant in 1-inch squares to a flat filled with an all-purpose potting mix. Keep the flat moist until small ferns appear. These can be planted in individual pots when they reach 2 to 3 inches in height.

Specialty Gardens

As you become more confident of your skills in raising houseplants, you will likely become interested in special plants and indoor gardens for your home.

Once you've discovered the joy of growing plants indoors, you'll want to branch out from tried-and-true favorites and explore the possibilities of different kinds of indoor gardens. This chapter examines a variety of challenging plants and garden systems.

Many people have learned that blooming houseplants will bring the same grace and elegance to a home that cut flowers do, with the added advantage of lasting far longer. Other people prefer forcing bulbs, and even flowering branches, annuals, and perennials, into early bloom to bring a touch of springtime to drab winter months.

For the more ambitious, there are indoor gardens that can extend the growing seasons and expand the number of plants that can be grown in a small space. These range from miniature gardens in a bottle, to simple, passive hydroponic systems on a windowsill, to tiered light gardens in the corner of a basement, to elaborate temperature- and light-controlled freestanding greenhouses.

No matter what your interest or what you want to grow, this chapter will show you how you can do it in your own home.

This sunroom filled with potted plants and comfortable furniture is an inviting space for both plants and people.

An old-fashioned sunroom is home to potted houseplants and a contented cat.

FLOWERING HOUSEPLANTS

A flowering houseplant is a plant that produces flowers in an environment compatible with a home and its occupants. A flowering houseplant is further categorized by how it adapts to indoor conditions. Some plants, with care, do fine; others bloom only with help from you. Still others bloom indoors for a few weeks or months, then are discarded when blooms fade.

Many African violets (*Saintpaulia*) and begonias flower continually indoors for many years. These are truly the best of the indoor flowering plants. To keep them healthy and good-looking, meet their general care requirements and keep them in a stable setting.

Other plants, such as peace-lily (*Spathiphyllum*), kalanchoe (*Kalanchoe blossfeldiana*), Christmas cactus (*Schlumbergera*), or geranium (*Pelargonium*), flower either seasonally or intermittently throughout the year. Their usefulness indoors also lies in their attractiveness as foliage plants.

Plants such as the florist's gloxinia (*Sinningia speciosa*) require a rest period after they flower. Still other flowering plants are houseplants only when they flower. Such notables as chrysanthemum (*Chrysanthemum × morifolium*), Easter lily (*Lilium longiflorum*), and poinsettia (*Euphorbia pulcherrima*) fall into this category.

Encouraging Plants to Bloom

It's often necessary to coax your flowering houseplants to bloom by giving them a little more tender loving care and attention than usual. The intensity and duration of light are critical to flower production. Because flowering is a special energy-consuming activity, most plants require more light during this time than they need for maintenance. Often a plant that refuses to bloom isn't receiving enough light. A plant located near a north-facing window or door, where light is scarce, usually has difficulty blooming.

Certain plants flower only after exposure to a particular day length; this feature is called *photoperiodism*. When day length is longer than a specific minimum, plants referred to as "long-day plants" respond by moving into their flower-producing mode. Summer-blooming annuals are examples of long-day plants.

Other plants, referred to as "short-day plants," do just the reverse: They move into flower production when days are shorter than a certain maximum; that is, a specific number of daylight hours or less. Poinsettias (*Euphorbia pulcherrima*) are short-day plants. Interrupting the long dark period with just a few minutes of light will prevent flowering in short-day plants while it may permit flowering in long-day plants.

With most flowering plants from the florist, one season of bloom is all you can expect. It's doubtful that you'll be able to do much more with them than sustain their current flowers.

The plants will not flower again because the special greenhouse conditions required are so difficult to duplicate in the home.

Houseplants in flower generally need more water than usual, especially if you have placed them in a high-light, a high-heat, or a low-humidity situation, which spurs the plant to transpire more rapidly. Also make sure that your plants do not suffer from poor drainage. Most flowering houseplants prefer slightly dry roots before they'll produce buds. Once a plant has been induced to flower, it should be watered thoroughly and regularly. Pay special attention to its watering needs at this time.

A bougainvillea and a low, spreading variegated ivy (Hedera helix) *grace the top of this Victorian dressing table.*

A Hiemalis begonia (Begonia × hiemalis), baskets, and wax fruit create a three-dimensional still life on the shelf of a kitchen etagere.

During the flowering period plants need fertilizer with a higher proportion of phosphorous, the nutrient that increases bud formation. Some fertilizers are specifically formulated for flowering plants.

Pruning and shaping enhance flower production, but don't get carried away with the job and prune so much or so often that no buds can form. Plants also need to be pinched back after blossoming.

Finally, keep blooming plants out of direct sunlight, drafts, and hot, dry air currents. Flower petals cannot replenish lost moisture as easily as leaves can. Petals may burn, fade, or wilt under hot, dry conditions.

Dealing with Reluctant Bloomers

If you have provided all these environmental conditions and your plants still don't flower, consider the following questions:

Is the plant in a container that is too large for its roots?

A pot-bound houseplant is more likely to flower because it has little room to develop roots. All the energy that would have gone into root production is now invested in growth above ground.

Has the plant been transplanted recently?

Transplanting disrupts the plant's normal growing routine and also will give the roots more room to grow. Instead of transplanting just before flowering occurs, replace the top third of the potting mix with new mix.

Is the plant immature?

New plants may simply be too young to produce flowers. Some plants take years to reach maturity.

Is the potting mix pH either below 5.0 or above 8.0?

If the pH is 5.0 or below, certain toxic ions become available to the plant and impair its growth. A pH reading above 8.0 makes some micronutrients, such as iron and manganese, unavailable for healthy plant growth.

Is your plant in its dormant period?

Be patient. Don't try to rush this process; a plant needs to rest before it can flower.

When all else fails, try cutting back on water. The plant will often respond to this threat by producing flowers, which are its method of reproduction. Let the plant become dry, but don't continue the treatment if it wilts severely and no buds appear. Once buds appear, resume normal care and don't disorient the plant by moving it.

Caring for Plants After They Flower

Many plants require a rest immediately after flowering. Gradually begin watering less frequently, though no less deeply, over a period of a few weeks, and do not fertilize during this time.

It's easy to tell when a plant is past its flowering prime: The flowers fade and no new buds form. It will not come back into bloom unless it is pruned and possibly repotted. Allow the plant to dry out a bit, and do not repot at this time. Let the plant rest until the next flowering cycle.

There's a temptation to cut back the foliage of bulbous plants once the flowers have faded. However, many bulbous plants need their foliage to produce food reserves for the next flowering cycle. Yellowing foliage naturally signals the onset of dormancy; remove the foliage then.

FORCING BULBS

One rewarding aspect of indoor gardening is that you can persuade plants to bloom out of season. By duplicating—but shortening—the stages bulbs go through in your garden, you can

Flowering bulbs are easy to force into bloom indoors, where they add bright color to a home.

have tulips, daffodils, and hyacinths blooming in the house while the wind drifts snow outdoors or winter rains keep you out of your garden.

How to Force Hardy Bulbs

It's easy to force tulips, daffodils, hyacinths, and the little bulbs—crocuses and grape hyacinths—to bloom indoors ahead of their normal time outdoors. Grow them as Christmas gifts for friends, or plan a display to brighten January and February days.

Begin by buying the largest bulbs you can find of the type you wish to grow. Most retail nurseries and garden centers carry bulbs for forcing in fall. For those bulbs you can't find in your local store, use mail-order catalogs. Order by September so that the bulbs will be delivered in early fall. If you can not plant the bulbs

Bulb Varieties for Forcing

Type	Color	Flowering Time	Type	Color	Flowering Time
Crocus			**Narcissus** (*continued*)		
Flower Record	Purple	Late winter, spring	Ice Follies	Cream cup, white perianth	Winter and spring
King of the Striped	Striped	Winter and spring	Joseph MacLeod	Yellow	Winter
Peter Pan	White	Winter and spring	Magnet	Yellow trumpet, white perianth	Spring
Pickwick	Striped	Winter and spring			
Purpureus Grandiflorus	Purple	Winter and spring	Mt. Hood	White	Winter and spring
Remembrance	Purple	Winter and spring	Paper-white	White	Winter and spring
Victor Hugo	Purple	Winter and spring	Peeping Tom	Dwarf yellow	Winter
Yellow Mammoth	Yellow	Spring	Soleil d'Or	Yellow	Winter and spring
Hyacinthus			Tête à Tête	Dwarf yellow	Winter and spring
Amethyst	Violet	Spring	Unsurpassable	Yellow	Winter and spring
Amsterdam	Pink	Winter and spring	Van Sion	Double yellow	Late winter and spring
Anne Marie	Pink	Winter			
Bismarck	Blue	Winter	**Tulipa**		
Blue Giant	Blue	Winter	Attila	Lavender	Winter
Blue Jacket	Blue	Spring	Bellona	Yellow	Winter
Carnegie	White	Spring	Bing Crosby	Red	Winter and spring
Delft Blue	Blue	Winter	Charles	Red	Winter
Eros	Pink	Winter and spring	Christmas Marvel	Pink	Winter
Jan Bos	Red	Winter	Electra	Double red	Spring
Lady Derby	Pink	Winter	Golden Eddy	Red variegated with yellow or cream	Spring
L'Innocence	White	Winter			
Madame Krüger	White	Winter and spring	Hibernia	White	Winter and spring
Marle	Blue	Spring	Karel Doorman	Red variegated with yellow or cream	Winter
Marconi	Pink	Spring			
Ostara	Blue	Winter and spring	Kees Nelis	Red variegated with yellow or cream	Winter
Pink Pearl	Pink	Winter and spring			
Queen of the Pinks	Pink	Spring	Merry Widow	Red and white	Winter
Iris Reticulata and **Iris Dandordibe**			Mr. van der Hoef	Double yellow	Spring
Cantab	Blue	Winter and spring	Monte Carlo	Yellow	Winter
Danfordiae	Yellow	Winter	Olaf	Red	Winter and spring
Harmony	Blue	Winter and spring	Orange Blossom	Double pink	Spring
Hercules	Purple	Winter and spring	Orange Monarch	Orange	Winter and spring
Joyce	Blue	Winter and spring	Paul Richter	Red	Winter
J. S. Dijt	Lavender	Winter and spring	Peach Blossom	Double pink	Spring
Muscari (**Grape Hyacinth**)			Peerless Pink	Pink	Winter
Blue Spike	Double blue	Winter and spring	Plaisir	Greigii, red and white	Winter and spring
Early Giant	Blue	Winter and spring	Preludium	Pink	Winter
Narcissus			Prince Charles	Lavender	Winter
Barrett Browning	Orange cup/white perianth	Winter and spring	Princess Irene	Orange	Late winter and spring
Bridal Crown	Double yellow/ orange center	Winter and spring	Prominence	Red	Late winter
			Red Riding Hood	Greigii, red	Late winter and spring
Carlton	Yellow	Winter			
Chinese Sacred Lily	White	Winter and spring	Schoonoord	Double white	Spring
Dutch Master	Yellow	Winter and spring	Stockholm	Red	Winter
February Gold	Dwarf yellow	Winter and spring	Thule	Yellow and red	Winter
Geranium	White/orange cup	Spring	Willemsoord	Double red and white	Spring

immediately after their arrival, store them opened in a cool (35° to 55° F) place.

Prepare a growing medium of equal parts potting mix, builder's sand, and peat moss. To each 5-inch pot of this mix, add 1 teaspoon bonemeal. (For instructions on creating your own potting mix, see page 19.) If you don't want the bother of mixing your own, buy an all-purpose potting mix and add bonemeal.

The pot size depends on the type and quantity of the bulbs. One large daffodil or tulip bulb can be planted in a 4- or 5-inch pot in which three crocuses or other smaller bulbs would otherwise fit. For six tulips, daffodils, or hyacinths, you'll need an 8- to 10-inch pot. When you plant these large bulbs, cover the tops of tulips and hyacinths with an inch of potting mix; however, do not cover the necks and tops of daffodils. Cover the smaller bulbs, such as crocuses, with an inch of potting mix. Water bulbs thoroughly. (It is also possible to purchase preplanted containers of bulbs conditioned to begin the forcing process.)

Bulbs need a period of coolness after potting so that they can form a vigorous root system. Find a cool, frost-free place where bulbs can be forced. A garage that is attached to the house, but not heated, is a good place for bulbs to form roots. A cool attic or basement also will do. A temperature range of 35° to 55° F will promote root growth. Keep the potting mix evenly moist throughout this period.

You can start forcing the bulbs when sprouts begin to push up through the potting mix. Bring the pots indoors, a few each week, so that you will have blooms over a longer period of time, and place them in a sunny, cool (55° to 70° F) spot.

Never allow the potting mix to dry out. The cooler the air, the longer the flowers will last. Keep bulbs away from sources of heat, such as radiators and gas heaters. Bring all pots into a warm and sunny location by late February.

After the flowers fade, keep the foliage in good health by providing moisture and sunlight. As soon as any danger of hard freezing is past, move them to an out-of-the-way place outdoors where the foliage can continue to mature and store up strength for another year's blooms. Although the bulbs will not stand forcing a second year, you will find them useful additions to the outdoor garden. Plant them there when you bring them out from the house, or leave them in pots until the following autumn, transferring them then to the open ground.

Problems in forcing bulbs are few, but here are some that might occur.

• Tulips sometimes have aphids, either on the leaves when they emerge, or on the flower buds. For controls, see page 38.

• Flower buds of forced bulbs will blast (fail to open) if the potting mix is allowed to dry out severely after they've begun to grow.

• Sometimes bulbs have basal rot; this is seldom your fault. If the foliage suddenly turns yellow and stops growing, give it a gentle tug. Chances are you'll find it loose in the pot, attached to a rootless rotted bulb. Burn the bulb to destroy it and prevent the disease from spreading to other plants.

Forcing Tender Narcissus

No matter where you live, tazetta daffodils, also known as tender narcissus ('Paper-white' is the best-known cultivar), are delightful subjects for forcing indoors in a semisunny to sunny location. The bulbs are available in autumn at nurseries. Plant them in moist pebbles in a bowl, or pot them in a mixture of equal parts potting mix, sand, and peat moss kept moist. Either way, place the bases of the bulbs to a depth of 1 to 1½ inches, then water thoroughly. Drain and set in a cool (50° to 65° F), dark place until the roots form. Keep the pebbles or potting mix moist.

After the bulbs have a good root system—which usually takes two to four weeks—they may be brought into warmth and bright sun. Here they will quickly send up fragrant clusters of white or gold blossoms.

Discard tender narcissus after forcing if you live where winter cold dips below 20° F. In warmer climates, plant them in the garden outdoors. But don't try to force them again. Buy new stock each year for forcing.

Forcing Prepared Hyacinths and Crocus

A hyacinth or crocus bulb that has been pretreated will grow in water if placed in a specially designed container or jar, or in any vase that will hold the bulb in the top and allow the roots to reach into the bottom section. Fill the vase with water so that the base of the bulb is just above the water level. Add water as needed, and change the water every three to four weeks.

Top: The arching grace of these Paper-whites (Narcissus) *echoes the shape of the window in which they sit. Bottom: Adding blooming plants can brighten even a winter-drab room.*

A small piece of charcoal in the water will keep it sweet and prevent harmful bacteria from developing. Place in a dark, cool area until roots have formed (about 14 weeks) before moving to light. Use any of the varieties listed on page 58.

CREATING A LIGHT GARDEN

Proper light is one of the main secrets to growing healthy plants. Unfortunately, it is not necessarily available in all indoor situations. In addition, even exposures that are sufficiently bright in summer may be too dim to maintain growth and flowering during the winter months. This has led many amateur growers to try artificially lighting their plants to encourage growth, and one result of these experiments is the light garden.

Although theoretically a light garden can be defined as any growing area lit by artificial means, the term has, over time, evolved to mean the technique of growing plants under fluorescent lights. This technique is becoming increasingly popular because plants not only grow and flower extremely well under fluorescent lights, but also because the lamps are inexpensive to purchase and operate. They give off little heat and, unlike most other plant lights, are not glaring, making it possible to integrate light gardens into living areas. What's more, a single fluorescent light fixture can create a 2- by 4-foot growing space, far more space than is available in the average window.

For even more growing space, fixtures can be superimposed, giving enough room for a veritable indoor garden in one corner of a room. And since no natural light is needed, even a basement or closet space can be converted into a light garden.

Setting Up a Light Garden

The main element of any light garden is the light itself. Fluorescent lights are available in many configurations, but the most practical are four fixtures of two- to four-tube 40-watt lamps. Shop fixtures are preferred by hobbyists because they have built-in reflectors to direct light toward the plants. However, strip lighting (the common commercial type) can be easily adapted to light gardening by adding strips of white-painted cardboard or wood along the side of the fixture to direct light downward.

The simplest setup for a beginning light gardener is to suspend a fluorescent fixture over a tabletop by attaching chains to the ceiling. The lamp can then be easily adjusted to the desired height, and the equipment needed is relatively minor. The disadvantage of this setup is that the arrangement is not easily moved and may not blend well with the rest of the room.

If you want to grow many plants in a small space, a more elaborate arrangement of tiered shelves is ideal. They can be purchased ready-made from indoor gardening specialists, but many hobby growers prefer to build their own of wood or PVC (polyvinyl chloride) piping, which is readily available at building supply centers. Other alternatives includes standard shelf support systems, which are easily installed, and metal racking. Both should be at least 4 feet long. Light fixtures can even be inserted into existing furniture, such as bookshelves. In any situation, the light fixture can be suspended from the bottom of a shelf directly above or from the ceiling.

In setting up your own light garden, leave approximately 16 inches between shelves to start, but provide some means of adjusting the light fixture heights in the future, to allow for plant growth. A three-tiered light garden might feature one shelf at 12 inches for small plants and seedlings, one at 16 inches for medium-sized plants, and one at 24 inches for taller plants.

Plants should be set under light fixtures so that the tops of their leaves are 6 to 12 inches from the light source. Since not all plants are of equal height, low-growing ones can be raised on inverted pots to bring them closer to the lights. Plants that are too close to the lights will burn. Plants that are too far away will have sparse and elongated foliage.

Fluorescent lamps, especially strip lighting, do not always come with electric cords and plugs, but these can be easily installed. Only grounded plugs should be used, to prevent electrical shocks. Light gardens, unless very extensive, will not require any electrical rewiring: They use little electricity and can simply be plugged into regular grounded outlets.

Although fluorescent tubes that have been designed for growing plants are available, ordinary fluorescent tubes are sufficient. One popular combination is to alternate inexpensive cool white and warm white tubes in the same fixture. Specialist growers of orchids, cacti,

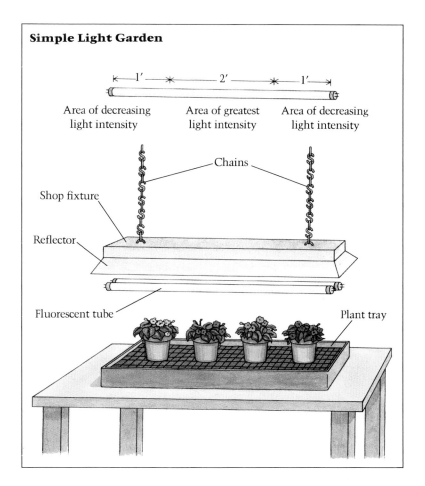

Simple Light Garden

←— 1' —→ ←— 2' —→ ←— 1' —→

Area of decreasing light intensity   Area of greatest light intensity   Area of decreasing light intensity

Chains

Shop fixture

Reflector

Fluorescent tube

Plant tray

bromeliads, and miniature roses might want to experiment with full-spectrum tubes for better growth and bloom.

One device well worth purchasing is a timer. These can be set on 12- to 16-hour days (14 hours of light is ideal for most plants). One timer is sufficient for a bank of several fluorescent fixtures. Just make sure that the timer is rated for more than the total wattage of all the fixtures being used.

Light gardens are surprisingly inexpensive to operate. A standard fixture of two 40-watt tubes plus a 20-watt ballast (the control box hidden inside such fixtures) uses only 100 watts of electricity, the same as a single 100-watt incandescent light, and it provides far more light!

Choosing Plants for a Light Garden

Almost any plant can be grown and will even bloom under lights, but low-growing plants are generally preferred. It is difficult to correctly light tall plants in a light garden: The upper leaves get all the light and the lower ones are left in shade. Plants that form flat rosettes do particularly well under lights, since all their leaves are equidistant from the lamps. Popular families for growing under lights include begonias, gesneriads, such as African violet (*Saintpaulia*) and flame-violet (*Episcia cupreata*), orchids, bromeliads, succulents, and jungle cacti. A kitchen light garden can be kept filled with fresh herbs and fast-growing vegetables such as lettuce and radishes. Terrariums also adapt extremely well to light gardens, and many people use lights to overwinter or grow bonsais.

The typical two-tube setup gives off enough light for most indoor plants to grow well, but some plants need stronger light. Such is the case for orchids, miniature roses, geraniums, and desert cacti, all of which do better under four-tube setups. Fruiting vegetables, such as tomatoes and cucumbers, also need maximum amounts of light to do well.

Fluorescent light gardens are ideal for starting seeds and cuttings of both indoor and outdoor plants. For dense growth, place the seed trays within a few inches of the light fixture, gradually lowering the trays as the plants grow so that they don't touch the tubes. Cuttings do not need a great deal of light and root well even if placed at the ends of the tubes.

Maintaining a Light Garden

Light gardening is an intensive method of growing plants. Most plants will not only grow more rapidly under lights, but will also bloom more abundantly and for longer periods of time. This kind of high performance will therefore require extra care.

You'll find that potting mixes dry out more quickly under lights than in the average indoor setting, and that you'll need to water more frequently. Also, for top performance the year around, a constant feed method is often best (see page 32). Once a month, leach the potting mix thoroughly by holding the pot under the tap and letting clear water run through it. Activities such as repotting and taking cuttings, which are usually done in spring or summer in a typical home setting, can be carried out the year around under lights.

Light intensities are highest nearer the lamps, so that full-sun plants can be placed there and shade-loving plants at a greater distance. Light intensities are also greatest directly under the tubes and toward their centers and weakest at the edges of the lamps and at their ends, so plants can be placed accordingly. Often, flowering plants, which generally require the most light, are grown near the center of the tubes, with foliage plants at either end of the fixture.

Fluorescent tubes are most intense when first used; they settle down to a relatively constant performance for about 12 to 18 months. Some hobbyists routinely replace all the tubes at the end of the year; others wait until the ends of the tube begin to blacken, a sign that they are wearing out. If both tubes in a fixture stop functioning at once or begin to flicker, it is likely that one of the two has burned out and should be changed. Keep tubes clean, since dust and water spotting can reduce light intensity considerably.

Fluorescent lights give off far less heat than other artificial light sources; furthermore, the heat is spread out over the entire length of the tube. Nevertheless, plants that touch them will burn, and fixture heights should be adjusted periodically to prevent this. During the summer months, when even a slight bit of extra heat is unwanted, ventilation may be required. Some growers simply adjust their timers at this time of year so that the lights come on during the night, when it is coolest, and turn off during the heat of the day.

CREATING A HYDROPONIC GARDEN

Conventional thought has always been that plants need soil in which to grow, yet scientists have known for generations that this isn't so. What plants need to grow are air, water, minerals, and some sort of anchoring mechanism. Soil helps provide these in nature, but there are many other possibilities when you are growing plants indoors.

Hydroponics, also called hydroculture, literally means growing plants in water. In fact, plants raised hydroponically are rarely grown in water alone, but instead use a support mechanism other than soil, often pebbles, gravel, or expanded clay pellets, to hold them up. The support product is called an aggregate. But the essential feature of a hydroponic garden is that water must necessarily contain all the nutrients needed for growth since the aggregate is inert. And air, essential to root growth, is provided through the rise and fall of water in the growing unit and helped along by the ample open spaces in the aggregate.

The advantages of hydroponic culture are numerous. First, it eliminates the need to have to deal with soils and potting mixes. Some people who are allergic to the microbes found in potting soils and may have even been told that they are allergic to plants find that they can grow plants without any harmful reaction. Soil-borne insects and diseases diminish when hydroponics are used. Also, people who tend to be negligent with their plants will find that with this system the plants basically take care of themselves.

The main reason that people use hydroponic systems, though, is as a time-saving device. When properly set up, most systems require no human intervention for two to three weeks. People who can't keep up a regular care schedule often find that only hydroponic systems offer them the autonomy they need.

Hydroponic systems do have negative aspects, though. Purchasing the materials needed to get started—special pots, aggregates, fertilizers, and so on—is quite expensive, although it becomes less so in the long run, since all the parts can be recycled. Hydroponics supplies are often hard to find locally and may have to be purchased by mail. Furthermore, plants are rarely sold in hydroponic systems: You have to do the work of acclimating them to hydroponics yourself.

Setting Up a Hydroponic Garden

There are essentially two methods of hydroponics for indoor use: passive methods, in which plant roots actually grow in water, and active or automated systems, in which water is pumped or poured through the aggregate on a regular basis.

Passive systems These are currently the most popular for growing decorative houseplants. A basic kit consists of an outer container with no drainage hole; a culture pot or insert full of perforations for improved air circulation, which fits into the outer container; an aggregate (generally clay pellets); and a water level indicator. The plant, washed of all its potting mix, is placed in the culture pot and the space around it is filled with aggregate. It is then thoroughly rinsed and set into the outer

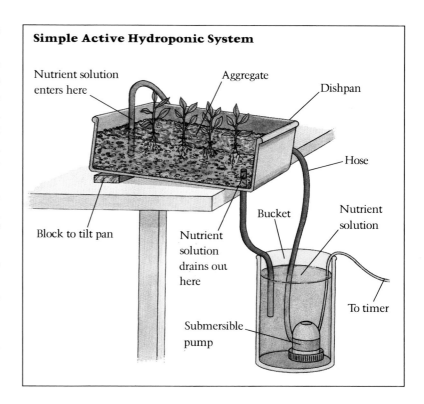

Simple Active Hydroponic System

Nutrient solution enters here

Aggregate

Dishpan

Hose

Block to tilt pan

Nutrient solution drains out here

Bucket

Nutrient solution

To timer

Submersible pump

container. Enough water is added to raise the water level on the reservoir indicator to half full.

The growing method couldn't be easier: Simply wait until the indicator reads empty, then fill the reservoir up to the halfway mark again. The reservoir should be filled to its maximum level only in the case of a prolonged absence.

Kits for passive hydroponics can be purchased as such, but it is also possible to adapt ordinary pots. Just set the pots with ample drainage holes in waterproof trays. Fill the tray up halfway, then let it drain before filling it up again.

Active systems There are practically as many automated hydroponic systems as there are hydroponic enthusiasts, but the basic principle is very simple: A nutrient solution is pumped regularly through an aggregate in a culture pot and drained away immediately. This brings in more oxygen than passive systems and allows for faster growth. Active systems are especially popular for plants where fast growth and production are required, such as indoor vegetables and herbs. In order to maintain the desired speed of growth, artificial light is also generally applied, since natural sunlight is rarely sufficient.

Complete kits for active systems are sold through specialized hydroponic outlets, but a simple system can be set up in a few hours using just a submersible pump, a bucket, two sections of hose or tubing, a plastic dishpan, and sufficient aggregate to fill the dishpan.

Start by cutting a hole at one end of the bottom of a dishpan that is just large enough for the end of the tube to fit into. Seal the hose into place with epoxy glue, making sure that there are no leaks, and set the pan on a table with the end with the hose hanging over the edge and the opposite end slightly raised, letting the hose drop down into a bucket placed on the floor.

Connect one end of the second section of hose to the pump and bring its opposite end back up to the far end of the pan, holding it in place with aggregate as you fill the pan. Fill the bucket with water and begin testing, setting the pump speed at its lowest setting at first, then increasing it if necessary. When water flows smoothly through the aggregate without splattering and drains back into the bucket, where it is again recirculated, the system is operational and plants can be added.

If the pump seems too powerful, the hose can be pinched at some point along its length to reduce the pressure. Since continuous pumping is not really required, you should consider adding a timer so that the system will automatically come on twice a day (three or four times in hot weather).

Planting a Hydroponic Garden

Any plants introduced into a hydroponic system must be completely cleaned of any potting mix particles beforehand. This is most easily done by starting with cuttings, but established plants can also be used if their root systems are thoroughly rinsed so all potting mix is removed. Younger plants normally adapt better to the change than older ones.

There are hydroponic aggregates with smaller particles that are especially designed for cuttings, but you can often root plants in regular aggregate just by keeping the water level higher than normal for the first two weeks. Seedlings can be started in vermiculite and transferred into hydroponics when well established.

All new transplants should be given special care for the first 10 days or so: Daily mistings can be helpful, but it is easier to cover them with a clear plastic tent.

Do not add nutrient solutions to newly planted hydroponic units. Wait until the plants show some signs of growth first, and then use a fertilizer specifically formulated for use in hydroponic systems.

Maintaining a Hydroponic Garden

Hydroponic gardens, while not as labor-intensive as maintaining plants in containers, do require some periodic maintenance. Perhaps the most important aspect is providing the essential nutrients for plant growth.

Regular fertilizers should be avoided, since they have been developed on the assumption that plants will be getting some of their nutrients from the soil in which they grow. Specialized hydroponic nutrients, with a balanced blend of minerals, including minor elements not included in most standard fertilizers, are required.

Perhaps the easiest nutrients to use with passive systems are those in the form of crystals or tablets designed to be added to the bottom of the container once every six months. Any residues left at that time should then be removed. Nutrients for active systems are usually designed to be added whenever the water level is topped up. The nutrient solution should be drained and replaced occasionally, according to the instructions on the nutrient label.

When vegetables mature in active systems, they should be harvested and the aggregate thoroughly rinsed and sterilized before reuse. The latter can be done by soaking the aggregate in a chlorine bleach solution (1 part chlorine, 9 parts water) for 24 hours, then running the system on water alone for a few days, changing the water frequently to remove any trace of chlorine.

Houseplants grown in a passive system rarely need repotting since their root system is not nearly as extensive in a water-based system as it would be in a potting mix. When the plant does become too top-heavy, it can simply be transplanted into a larger container. It is often easiest to place the old culture pot inside the new one, filling in the space between the two with aggregate, rather than to disturb the roots by trying to remove the old aggregate.

The root system of plants grown in passive systems should be leached every two to three months by rinsing with room-temperature water.

GROWING PLANTS IN A GREENHOUSE SETTING

Entering a greenhouse for the first time is like stepping into another world. It may be snowing outside, but inside a greenhouse you are transported to the steamy, languid tropics or springtime in the desert, surrounded by exotic orchids or lush displays of succulents.

Today's greenhouses and solariums are simple, practical, and no longer the domain of the wealthy. They can be freestanding structures, add-ons to the house, or window extensions over a kitchen sink or in a corner of a living room. A greenhouse can fit wherever you have space: in a window, on a balcony, in the backyard, or even on the roof.

The term *greenhouse* refers to any structure that traps and stores energy by means of transparent panels. In common parlance, however, a greenhouse is a structure specifically designed to have as much transparent surface as possible oriented toward the sun. A sun porch, a sunroom, or even a sunny window can provide some of the benefits of a greenhouse.

Types of Greenhouses

Freestanding greenhouses are what most people mean when they mention greenhouses. These are separate buildings, built to any size and covered with glass, acrylic, or fiberglass.

Solariums, or *sunrooms*, provide an indoor-outdoor living space, and are as effective as a greenhouse for plants that enjoy plenty of direct light. A solarium is ideal for sun lovers—plants and people—yet both can suffer from too much sun if there are no blinds or screens to control the intensity of light, especially in a south-facing solarium.

Greenhouse additions are one of the latest trends in indoor growing spaces. Unlike a solarium, designed primarily for use by people, the greenhouse addition is a space devoted to plants first. It is usually smaller and more intimate than a solarium, and is seen not so much as a room of its own but as an extension of the one to which it is attached. The kitchen is a perfect room for a greenhouse addition.

Greenhouse windows are well within most budgets and space constraints. Kits are available that will fit standard windows and can be installed in as little as one afternoon. Choose a window with a view you won't miss, since the plant-filled greenhouse will block the view.

There is an extremely simple alternative to even the window greenhouse. Miniature indoor greenhouses can be placed on a windowsill or on a shelf under lights. These have many uses: propagating new plants, curing ailing plants that have been suffering from insufficient humidity, isolating sick plants during treatment, and forcing flowering plants to bloom. They can also make attractive permanent homes for humidity-loving tropical species.

Choosing Plants for a Greenhouse

How different can growing plants in a greenhouse be from growing them in a house? Quite a bit, actually. Glassed-in structures, whether they're true greenhouse additions, solariums, or only greenhouse windows, are inevitably more exposed to temperature extremes than indoor environments, from heat in summer to cold nights in winter, and the sunlight they receive is more intense. Humidity can also be much higher. Furthermore, seasonal variations are likely to be felt more clearly. Inevitably, these differences will help you determine the choice of the plants you grow.

Visiting public greenhouses will often give you some idea of new plants that can be tried. Any greenhouse collection should also include a few winter-blooming plants, such as holiday cactus (*Schlumbergera*), kalanchoe, and Rieger begonias (*Begonia* $\times$ *hiemalis*), whose off-season color will be especially appreciated.

This greenhouse room includes a work space for caring for plants. Adjustable shades let the owners adjust the light and heat within the room.

A greenhouse window is the perfect setting for growing plants.

Many greenhouse spaces are used as nurseries during the winter and spring months. Spring-flowering bulbs are easily forced in greenhouses for bloom during the winter, and outdoor perennials, such as hostas and lilies-of-the-valley, can be brought inside for the winter where they will bloom months ahead of schedule. A greenhouse space can also become a winter holding-over space for tender plants that spend the summer outside.

There are practically no houseplants you cannot grow in a warm greenhouse, although shade lovers may need to be protected from full sun by being placed on lower benches or behind more sun-resistant plants. Keep in mind that tropical plants such as African violets (*Saintpaulia*) and crotons (*Codiaeum variegatum*) should be kept in the home if warm winter temperatures cannot be assured.

Caring for Greenhouse Plants

It is important to determine, at the very start, whether you want a warm greenhouse, where winter nighttime temperatures never drop below 55° to 70° F, or a cool greenhouse, where temperatures can drop as low as 40° to 50° F; this will determine, to a large extent, the kind of plants you will be able to grow.

Even within a cool greenhouse, though, there are inevitably spots that are warmer than the others, allowing you to grow tropical plants. Similarly, cooler spots will be found near exposed areas of a warm greenhouse, meaning that you can, to a certain degree, grow both subtropical and tropical plants in the same space.

Greenhouse plants generally follow the seasons quite closely, growing and blooming abundantly during the spring and summer and going dormant or semidormant in fall and winter. They will need abundant, perhaps even daily, watering during the growing season, whereas especially in cool greenhouses they may need little or no watering for long periods in winter.

Cool greenhouse plants should be fertilized regularly from late winter through summer, then allowed to harden off by stopping fertilization altogether in early fall. Warm greenhouse plants follow a similar pattern, but still require light fertilizing during the fall and winter.

The close proximity of plants in a greenhouse environment can lead to sudden outbursts of

Orchids are one family that can be grown to a much greater extent and with more success in a greenhouse than in a home. Cattleyas, dendrobiums, miltonias, vandas, and many others thrive there. In fact, there are very few orchids that will not thrive in a home greenhouse.

Desert cacti and succulents are perhaps among the easiest plants to grow in greenhouse conditions. They don't mind the often extreme heat and light of the summer months, and many actually require winter nighttime temperatures between 40° and 50° F, the kind that occur quite naturally in cool greenhouses, in order to bloom. Since little supplementary heat is needed to grow them, they are extremely economical choices as well.

Many greenhouse owners find themselves using their structures for growing edible plants. Vegetables, which rarely thrive on a windowsill, do wonderfully in the warmth, humidity, and light of a greenhouse. Herbs of all kinds will thrive in a greenhouse environment, and tropical and subtropical fruits, including everything from citrus to kiwis to bananas, can also be grown with ease.

insect infestation; high humidity levels there can lead to the rapid spread of diseases such as mildew and blight. Control methods should therefore be applied as soon as the first symptom is noted, and quarantining new plants is a must. Many people prefer to close their greenhouse spaces down during the hot months of summer and place the plants in the outdoor garden. This is an ideal moment for a general cleanup. Cleaning both improves light penetration and helps prevent disease and insect infestations during the winter months.

Humid air condensing on greenhouse coverings during the winter leads to cold water dripping onto plants, resulting in physical damage or disease. Special anticondensation coverings are available to help prevent this, and sprays with similar effects can be applied to many nontreated greenhouse films. It is often just as simple to tack up a temporary inner shell of clear polyethylene for the winter months.

The extreme intensity of sunlight, especially after an extended period of cloudy weather, can cause burning of delicate plant parts. This rarely kills plants, but damaged tissue will not recover and the plant may remain unsightly for many months. Always acclimate new plants slowly before putting them near the glass. Shade-loving plants should be kept permanently under benches or behind more tolerant varieties. Many greenhouse owners install shade cloth, applied to the inside or the outside of the structure, to provide extra protection during the summer months.

A greenhouse addition can add light and warmth to a room even when snow covers the ground outside.

Gallery of Houseplants

Making a selection from among the hundreds of different houseplants available today can be downright bewildering if not discouraging, especially if you are unfamiliar with plants or undecided about what you want and can grow. This gallery of distinctive houseplants will help you sort through the multitude of plants available.

The range of houseplants is enormous, and this look at some possibilities for an indoor garden lists only a few of the many thousands available. An attempt has been made to list not only favorites, but also more unusual plants that you might want to grace your home.

The entries are organized alphabetically according to botanical names. Common names are listed beneath the botanical. Should you know only the common name of a plant, you can find the botanical counterpart in the index on pages 106 and 107. Each listing features a general discussion of the group and its care requirements, followed by brief descriptions of the many species and varieties readily available. Beyond serving as a selection guide, the information included with each entry will aid you in the care of your houseplant.

Just as paintings in an art gallery may be hung with other paintings of a similar period, we have placed some plant families with the same care requirements together. These sections, for Begonias, Bromeliads, Desert Cacti, Ferns, Orchids, Palms, Philodendrons, and Succulents, are listed in alphabetical order throughout the gallery.

An all-purpose mix is recommended for each plant unless otherwise specified. Information on potting mixes begins on page 19.

Whether you're a beginning gardener or have greater experience, there's sure to be a houseplant to suit your every need.

Abutilon hybridum

Aeschynanthus 'Flash'

Aglaonema 'Silver Queen'

Abutilon

Abutilon, flowering maple, Chinese-lantern

This tropical viny shrub of the Hollyhock family is extremely vigorous, easily growing several feet in a year. The flowers have striking rocketlike shapes, and the maple-shaped leaves are sometimes dappled with yellow or white. Stems are most attractive espaliered or trained.

A. × *hybridum* (Chinese-lantern) produces white, yellow, salmon, or purple blooms. *A. megapotamicum* 'Variegata' (trailing abutilon) features red and yellow blossoms with large, pollen-bearing dark brown anthers. *A. pictum* 'Thompsonii' has yellow marbled leaves and bears an orange-salmon flower.

Provide bright direct light, moist potting mix, and average indoor humidity levels. Feed with each watering, more heavily in summer.

Temperature 68° to 72° F days; 50° to 60° F nights.

Water Keep potting mix very moist, but do not allow to stand in water.

Light Bright direct sunlight at least 4 hours a day, preferably near a south- or west-facing window.

Propagation Cuttings root easily in spring.

Potting mix All-purpose mix or 2 parts loam, 1 part peat moss, and 1 part coarse sand.

Repotting Repot in winter or early spring, as needed.

Grooming In winter, prune plant back to keep it 18 to 30 inches high. Keep to desired height and shape with light pruning or clipping at any time.

Aeschynanthus

Lipstick plant

This plant is most spectacular when suspended at eye level so that its trailing stems can show off their bright flowers. Put several plants together in one hanging container for a more striking effect. The lipstick plant, *A. lobbianus*, sometimes sold as *A. radicans*, features red blooms extending from a purplish calyx. *A. longicaulus*, previously sold as *A. marmoratus*, has attractively mottled waxy leaves and greenish flowers. The yellow to orange flowers of *A. speciosus* cluster at the ends of the stems.

These trailers need warmth and shade to do well under ordinary room conditions. Place in a bright spot away from direct sunshine and water regularly from spring to autumn. During the winter allow the plant to rest in a cool, dry spot. These plants prefer a high level of humidity.

Temperature 68° to 72° F days; 65° to 68° F nights. 60° F in winter.

Water Keep potting mix evenly moist during the growing season. Water sparingly in winter.

Light Bright indirect light.

Propagation Take stem cuttings in spring or summer.

Potting mix African violet mix.

Repotting Repot every 2 to 3 years in spring.

Grooming After flowering ceases prune back stems.

Aglaonema

Chinese evergreen

The Chinese evergreen is a favorite in homes around the world because it is tolerant of a wide range of conditions. The plant grows to 2 feet tall and has oblong, lance-shaped leaves 6 to 9 inches long and 2 to 3 inches wide. The waxy deep green leaves are marked with silver bars between pale lateral veins. The leaves of *A. crispum* are green and gray. *A. crispum* 'Silver Queen' has leaves that are primarily silver-white and cream with green edges and veins. *A. commutatum* has glossy leaves marked with green, yellowish green, or gray. *A. modestum* has solid leaves with no markings.

This plant tolerates both poor light and dry air. Place it in a moderately lit spot and keep the potting mix evenly moist. Feed lightly with each watering, more heavily in summer with a mild fertilizer solution. Though it will tolerate dry air, Chinese evergreen does prefer a humid environment, so place it on a humidifying tray if the air is particularly dry.

Anthurium scherzeranum

Aphelandra squarrosa

Temperature 70° to 80° F days; 60° to 65° F nights.

Water Keep evenly moist, drier in winter.

Light Moderate light; will tolerate low (reading-level) light. A north-facing window is best.

Propagation Root division or stem cuttings, or start seeds in spring and summer.

Repotting Blossoms best when pot bound.

Grooming Remove yellowed leaves.

Anthurium
Anthurium, flamingo-flower, tailflower

Anthuriums are among the best-known tropical flowers. The colored portion of the bloom is actually a bract; the tiny flowers appear on the spike, or spadix. New, ever-blooming varieties such as 'Lady Jane' and 'Southern Blush' are widely available. *A. scherzeranum* is a small species suitable for indoor culture.

Though anthuriums are generally grown for their flowers, some foliage varieties are becoming increasingly popular. *A. crystallinum*, which is often available, has heart-shaped emerald green leaves up to 12 inches across and 20 inches long, overlaid with silver veins. *A. hookeri* 'Alicia' has thick, leathery dark green leaves with wavy edges and extremely short petioles that form a bird's-nest rosette.

Keep anthuriums in humid air and fertilize lightly with each watering when they are actively growing.

Temperature 70° to 75° F days; 55° to 60° F nights.

Water Keep evenly moist. Let foliage types dry slightly before watering.

Light Provide at least 4 hours of curtain-filtered sunlight from a bright south, east, or west window.

Propagation Remove plantlets or rooted side shoots as they form.

Repotting Leave room at the top to mound up potting mix as crown develops. Repot infrequently.

Grooming Mound up potting mix as high crowns form. Remove aerial roots and pick off yellowed leaves.

Pests and problems Brown tips on stems result from dry air. Will not bloom if light is too low.

Aphelandra squarrosa
Aphelandra, zebra-plant

For 6 weeks in fall this favorite of Victorian conservatories provides an impressive display of color as large, conical, deep yellow flowers emerge from golden bracts. The rest of the year, this small, erect, evergreen shrub has dark, elliptical leaves striped with ivory veins, which creates a zebra effect. The variety 'Louisae' is compact, with relatively small leaves. 'Apollo White', 'Dania', and 'Brockfeld' are even more compact and produce leaves with the most striking vein patterns.

Aphelandras tend to become gangly. To combat this, cut back after flowering, letting 1 or 2 pairs of leaves remain. Feed lightly with each watering throughout the growing season, never allow the rootball to dry out, and keep the plant warm in winter. This plant needs a high level of humidity and will do best if placed on a humidifying tray.

Temperature 70° to 75° F days; 60° to 70° F nights.

Water Keep evenly moist and do not allow plant to dry out. Water less in winter.

Light Bright indirect light or filtered sun near a curtained window with an eastern or western exposure.

Propagation In spring, cut off a side shoot that has roots and plant in 2 parts peat moss and 1 part sand. Apply bottom heat until new growth begins.

Repotting Repot in winter or early spring, as needed.

Grooming In spring, cut back stem, leaving 1 or 2 pairs of healthy leaves.

Pests and problems Mealybugs may be a problem. Leaf drop usually results from potting mix that is too wet or too dry, cold air, or direct sun. Brown leaf tips result from low humidity.

Araucaria heterophylla
Norfolk Island pine

Symmetrical tiers of branches with needlelike leaves are

Araucaria heterophylla

Asparagus densiflorus 'Sprengeri'

featured on *A. heterophylla* (also known as *A. excelsa*). Trees range in size from those small enough to be displayed in a terrarium to very tall specimens suitable for placement in entryways or large rooms.

This conifer is easy to grow; nevertheless, it grows slowly, so be patient. Place it in a brightly lit, cool location with average indoor humidity levels. Keep the potting mix moist; protect the plant from hot, dry air; and feed lightly with each watering throughout the growing season. With proper care, it can eventually reach 10 to 15 feet tall indoors.

Temperature   55° to 65° F days and nights. Cooler in winter.

Water   Water regularly to keep evenly moist.

Light   Bright indirect light. Protect from direct sun in summer.

Propagation   Not recommended for home gardeners.

Repotting   Repot every 3 to 4 years. Keep pot bound to restrict growth.

Grooming   Pick off yellowed leaves.

Pests and problems   Mealybugs, spider mites, and scales may be a problem. Leaf drop and loss of lower branches is caused by hot, dry air or insufficient moisture in potting mix. Dropping of older leaves and lower branches is natural.

Asparagus
Asparagus fern

The two most popular asparagus plants, *A. setaceus* (sometimes sold as *A. plumosus*) and *A. densiflorus* 'Sprengeri', feature delicate, feathery foliage. Although these plants may look like ferns, the tiny leaves are actually flattened stems. *A. setaceus* is a trailing vine with 12- to 18-inch stems, covered with ⅛-inch dark green needles. *A. densiflorus* 'Sprengeri' has arching 18- to 24-inch stems that are covered with thousands of tiny, flat needles. Both look best displayed in hanging containers.

These plants have been favorites for generations because they are so easy to care for. Provide bright indirect or curtain-filtered light and average indoor humidity levels and feed lightly with each watering. Unlike true ferns, asparagus ferns will tolerate a wide range of temperatures, humidity levels, and light levels.

Temperature   Average: 68° to 72° F days; 60° to 65° F nights.

Water   Keep barely moist.

Light   Bright indirect or curtain-filtered sunlight.

Propagation   Divide thick, fleshy roots of old plants in any season.

Potting mix   All-purpose mix or 1 part loam, 1 part peat moss or leaf mold, and 1 part sharp sand.

Repotting   Any time plants become overcrowded.

Grooming   Pinch back stems to keep plant bushy. If plant gets leggy, cut stems back to potting mix level. Fresh new stems will soon grow.

Pests and problems   Leaves will turn yellow and drop if plant is suddenly moved to a new location with low light.

Aspidistra elatior
Cast-iron plant

This is one of the most famous houseplants of the Victorian era, noted for its ability to survive against considerable odds of extreme heat and low light that would be deadly to most other plants. The leaves are oblong, leathery, shiny, and dark green, growing 15 to 30 inches long and 3 to 4 inches wide. They intermingle above a clump of 6-inch-long stems. In spring, bell-shaped dark purple flowers are borne singly at the base of the plant.

This is a slow-growing, long-lasting plant that responds well to proper attention but survives poor treatment for a long time. Place out of direct sun; water and lightly feed regularly from spring to fall. Reduce water and keep cool during the winter. Dry air is generally not harmful, but keep plant out of drafts. Although the plant can withstand most abuse, it cannot endure soggy mix or frequent repotting.

Temperature   65° to 75° F days; 60° to 65° F nights.

Water   Keep evenly moist in spring and summer. Water sparingly during the winter.

Light   Moderate light. Tolerant of shade.

Propagation   Divide root crown in late winter to early spring.

Aspidistra elatior 'Variegata'

Begonia × semperflorens-cultorum

Begonia × rex-cultorum 'Cleopatra'

Repotting Only every 4 to 5 years in spring when plant is very crowded.

Grooming Wash leaves every 2 weeks.

Pests and problems Spider mites may be a problem.

Azalea

See *Rhododendron*

Begonias

With more than 1,500 known species, this plant family offers the indoor gardener a vast array of beautiful plants that are easily adapted to almost any indoor environment.

Flowering Begonias

These can be divided into several different categories. The popular wax or fibrous-rooted begonia (*B.* × *semperflorens*) has crisp, fleshy stems topped with waxy, heart-shaped leaves and flowers in a wide range of colors that bloom the year around. Choose from varieties with single, semidouble, or fully double flowers.

B. coccinea, the angelwing begonia, combines beautiful foliage with clusters of blooms in pink, red, orange, or white. They grow atop bamboolike stems swollen at the joints. The Kusler hybrids sold by begonia specialists are some of the best types of angel-wing begonias.

B. × *hiemalis* (Rieger begonia, hiemalis begonia, elatior begonia) is low growing and exceptionally bushy. Some of the newer cultivars have bronze or red foliage. The flowers, available in yellow, red, white, or orange, are generally large and double. Rieger begonias prefer cooler locations than most begonias.

Tuberous begonias (*B.* × *tuberhybrida*) produce the largest flowers of all begonias grown indoors. They are best displayed while blooming, then transplanted to the garden.

Foliage Begonias

Many other begonias are grown primarily for their foliage. Cane begonias have leaves borne vertically on erect, smooth stems with swollen nodes resembling those of bamboo. They are asymmetrical and quite diverse in color, size, and variegation. Although grown primarily for

their foliage, they will bloom intermittently with enough light.

Shrub begonias branch abundantly, hiding their stems from view. The bare-leaf types have smooth, metallic-looking leaves. These require more sunlight than other begonias. Another type of shrub begonia has leaves covered with thick hair or felt. These hairy-leaf begonias prefer diffuse light. The fern-leaf begonias (*B. foliosa*) are best known for their unusual foliage.

Rhizomatous begonias are the largest group of begonias, known for their striking foliage. Although old-fashioned hybrids can still be found, the smaller varieties, such as the tiny *B. boweri* (eyelash begonia) and *B. heracleifolia* (star begonia), are increasingly popular. *B. masoniana* (iron-cross begonia) produces large, bumpy, heart-shaped leaves in yellow-green with a dark burgundy Maltese-cross pattern in the center.

B. × *rex-cultorum* are a sizable group of plants grown primarily for their foliage, although they will bloom if

given good light. The leaves of most cultivars are large and have asymmetrical blades with diverse, brilliant coloration and textures.

Give plants plenty of bright light, a normal indoor temperature that drops slightly at night, and a light feeding with each watering while the plant is actively growing or flowering. Flowering begonias prefer high humidity; foliage types do well in average indoor humidity levels. Begonias are very sensitive to overwatering, so use a well-draining mix.

Care of Begonias

Temperature 65° to 80° F days; 65° to 70° F nights. Tuberous and Rieger begonias do well in 65° to 70° F days; 50° to 55° F nights.

Water Keep flowering begonias evenly moist and tuberous begonias very moist. Water foliage begonias when potting mix is dry to the touch.

Light Bright indirect light. An east or west exposure is best. Bare-leaf shrub begonias prefer some direct sun.

Brassaia actinophylla

Bromeliad: Aechmea fasciata

Bromeliad: Ananas comosus 'Variegatus'

Propagation From seed, stem, and leaf cuttings, or division of the rhizome.

Potting mix African violet mix or 1 part peat moss, 2 parts sphagnum moss, and 1 part perlite.

Repotting Repot most begonias only when growth is inhibited. Cut back and repot wax begonias when flowering finishes. Repot cane and shrub begonias annually in spring.

Grooming Pinch back young plants to prevent legginess and strengthen blossoms.

Pests and problems Mealybugs may be a problem. Watch for powdery mildew.

Brassaia actinophylla

Schefflera, umbrella tree

This elegant tree, also known as *Schefflera actinophylla*, is a fast-growing evergreen that can reach 8 feet in height. Its common name, the umbrella tree, derives from the glossy green leaflets that spread out like the sections of an umbrella. The leaves of young plants are 2 to 3 inches wide with 3 to 5 leaflets; eventually the leaves grow to be 18 inches across, composed of 16 leaflets.

This is a hardy, easy-to-care-for plant that can tolerate a certain amount of neglect. Place the plant in a bright spot and the container on top of a saucer of gravel with water to maintain humidity. Feed lightly with each watering throughout the growing season with a mild solution of 5-10-5 fertilizer.

Temperature 60° to 75° F days; 50° to 55° F nights.

Water Water thoroughly when potting mix is moderately dry.

Light Bright indirect light, but it benefits from 4 hours of direct sunlight daily.

Propagation Take stem cuttings at any time or air-layer in spring.

Repotting Repot when plant is crowded, any season.

Grooming Give an occasional shower and pick off yellowed leaves.

Pests and problems Highly susceptible to spider mites. Will get spindly and weak if light is too low.

Bromeliads

Many people have discovered that bromeliads, with their exotic foliage and showy flowers, are not difficult to grow indoors. The most distinctive feature of this group of more than 2,000 species is the rosette of leaves that forms a cup to hold the water that nourishes the plant. Flowers and large colorful bracts emerge from the center of some varieties. These bracts are modified leaves that grow from the same axils as the flowers.

Originally from the jungle, most bromeliads are epiphytes (air plants), growing suspended in trees and on rocks in their native habitat, and gathering moisture and food from rainfall and debris in the air. If you decide to keep them in pots, use a light potting mix that can drain easily. Bromeliads do well with average to high indoor humidity levels and should be fed lightly with each watering throughout the growing season.

Bromeliads also need lots of sun and high temperatures in order to bloom. If you're having trouble inducing your plant to bloom, place it in a plastic bag with a ripe apple for a few days. The ethylene gas from the apple will initiate flower buds. After the plant finishes flowering, the rosette enters into a slow dying process that can last as long as 3 years. Planting the offsets that form at the base of the plant will keep your collection blooming year after year.

Aechmea

Living-vaseplant, urnplant, coralberry

The most common of this group is *A. fasciata*, the living-vaseplant or urnplant. Its broad, thick leaves are mottled with stripes of gray and deep sea green; its conical rosette of pink bracts and large blue flowers creates a splendid visual effect. The upright rosette of thick, silver-banded leaves distinguishes the striking *A. chantinii*. Its flowers last for several months. *A. fulgens discolor*, commonly known as the coralberry, features broad leaves, green on top and purple underneath. The contrast in the foliage is heightened by the purple flower. The red berries

Bromeliad: Neoregelia carolinae 'Tricolor'

Bromeliad: Cryptanthus

Bromeliad: Billbergia

Bromeliad: Guzmania lingulata

Bromeliad: Vriesea splendens

that give the plant its common name form after the flower fades.

Ananas comosus

Pineapple, ivory pineapple

Pineapples are the fruit of *Ananas comosus*. You can grow one by simply cutting off a bit of the fruit along with the fruit's tuft, planting it in potting mix, and placing it in full sun. Narrow gray-green leaves, often with prickly ribbing running up the sides, form a striking rosette. The pineapple rarely produces flowers and fruit indoors. Many people believe that *A. comosus* 'Variegatus', the ivory pineapple, has much more attractive foliage.

Billbergia

Vaseplant, queen's-tears, foolproof plant

These are among the easiest bromeliads to grow, but they flower for only a short time. *B. nutans*, known as queen's-tears, has grasslike gray-green leaves. Amidst the foliage is an arching spray of pink and green flowers. *B. pyramidalis*, sometimes called the foolproof plant, sports a colorful

combination of long, straplike green leaves, bright red bracts tipped with violet, and upright scarlet flowers with yellow stamens. *B.* 'Fantasia' has green leaves heavily splotched with cream. The red bracts appear in fall or early spring.

Cryptanthus

Earthstars, rainbow-star, zebra-plant

Most often called earthstars because of the shape of the rosettes, these plants are small and have great variation in leaf color. *C. bivittatus* has green leaves with creamy white stripes. Its common hybrids include 'Starlite' and 'Pink Starlight'. *C. bromelioides* 'Tricolor', the rainbow-star, displays a colorful array of stripes down the length of its wavy leaves. *C. zonatus* (zebra-plant) resembles zebra skin, banded in ivory and tannish brown.

Guzmania

The vase-shaped rosettes of guzmanias can grow to 20 inches wide. The plants bloom from late winter to summer. The small true flowers are

surrounded by large, showy bracts in reds, yellows, and oranges. *G. lingulata* has brightly colored bracts ranging from red to yellow, and white flowers.

Neoregelia

Blushing bromeliad, painted-fingernail-plant

These produce some of the largest rosettes of any bromeliad, composed of thick, shiny leaves. When mature, *N. carolinae* 'Tricolor' (blushing bromeliad) reaches a diameter of 30 inches. Large, saw-toothed leaves, variegated in cream and green, jut out in an orderly arrangement. Just before flowering, the youngest leaves in the center turn bright red. *N. spectabilis* features green leaves with pink-tipped ends; hence its common name, the painted-fingernail-plant.

Vriesea

Vriesea, flaming-sword

This genus features many plants attractive for both their foliage and flowers. *V. splendens* forms a rosette of wide, purple-banded leaves. The common name, flaming-sword, refers to its flower—a long

spike of red bracts and yellow flowers.

Care of Bromeliads

Temperature Average constant temperatures of 65° to 70° F are fine for foliage types and plants in flower. Warmer temperatures, 75° to 80° F, are needed to initiate budding.

Water Always keep the cup of epiphytic or rosette-type bromeliads filled with water, preferably rainwater, and change it occasionally. Lightly spray these bromeliads with warm water regularly. Allow plants growing in pots to dry out, then water lightly so that they are barely moist. Overwatering and poor drainage will kill the plant.

Light Abundant light for most bromeliads. An east- or west-facing window is best. *Ananas* requires full sun; *Cryptanthus* and *Guzmania* prefer a less well-lit location.

Propagation Remove mature offsets and a good section of roots from larger plants and pot shallowly in a light mix. Keep warm.

Potting mix All-purpose mix that is light and well draining,

Caladium 'Red Flash'

Calathea louisae

commercial bromeliad or orchid mix, or 1 part osmunda fiber, 1 part peat moss or leaf mold, and 1 part coarse sand.

Repotting   Rarely necessary.

Grooming   Wash leaves occasionally.

Pests and problems   Scales and mealybugs can be a problem. Brown areas on leaves indicate sunburn. Brown tips on leaves result from dry air. Overwatering is fatal to these plants.

Caladium
Caladium

Dozens of varieties of caladium with different leaf patterns and colorings all can create a splendid display of color. Masses of paper-thin, heart-shaped leaves 12 to 24 inches long are borne on long stalks. The exquisite foliage of this perennial dies back for a 4-month period during dormancy. *C. × hortulanum* features leaves with a range of colors—green with red veins, or white and cream with pink or green veins. The edges may be flat, wavy, or ruffled. *C. humboldtii* is a miniature

plant with light green leaves splotched with white.

Bright indirect light or curtain-filtered sunlight is best. Keep the pot on a humidifying tray and mist daily while growing. Temperatures should never dip below 70° F during the day. Feed lightly with each watering throughout the growing season.

Temperature   75° to 80° F days; 60° to 70° F nights.

Water   Water regularly during growing season. Allow to dry out and become dormant in late fall.

Light   Bright indirect light or curtain-filtered direct sunlight.

Propagation   In fall, after the plant dries out, take tubers from the pot and store in dry peat moss at 50 to 60° F for 2 months. In spring, divide tubers and plant one tuber per 5-inch pot in all-purpose mix.

Repotting   Each year in spring.

Grooming   Trim faded foliage during the growing period. Cut off dead foliage in fall as the plant dies back.

Calathea
Calathea, peacock-plant

Calatheas have what many consider to be the most beautifully variegated foliage of any indoor plant. The stems are often red, and the large, blade-shaped leaves have various patterns of greens on top. Some cultivars have purples and reds on the undersides of the leaves. Calatheas will not tolerate dry air or drafts; grow in a lit terrarium or use a humidifier for best results. Feed lightly once a year in early spring if the plant is in a dimly lit spot. Otherwise, fertilize lightly with each watering throughout the summer. Plants can reach 2 feet high, with individual leaves 8 inches across.

Temperature   75° to 80° F days; 65° to 70° F nights.

Water   Keep very moist at all times, but do not allow to stand in water.

Light   Will survive low (reading-level) light.

Propagation   Divide older specimens.

Repotting   Repot at any time.

Grooming   Pick off yellowed leaves.

Pests and problems   Brown leaves result from dry air.

Callisia elegans
See *Tradescantia*

Chlorophytum comosum
Spiderplant

The familiar spiderplant has been grown indoors since nearly 200 years ago when Goethe, the German writer, first brought the plant inside to study. The spiderplant can grow to be a rotund 3 feet tall. Wiry stems up to 5 feet long, bearing plantlets, spring forth among arching grassy green leaves often striped with yellow or white. This plant is perfect for a hanging container.

The spiderplant will grow in almost any location—sun, shade, dry, or moist. Water freely from spring to autumn and keep in a moderate to cool location with average indoor humidity levels. Feed lightly with each watering while the plant is actively growing. The plantlets can be left on

Chlorophytum comosum 'Vittatum'

Chrysanthemum × *morifolium*

the stems of the mother plant for a full look or they can be removed for propagation. The plant will produce the most plantlets when slightly pot bound.

Temperature Moderate: 65° to 75° F days; 55° to 65° F nights.

Water Water liberally during the growing season, sparingly in winter.

Light Bright indirect light, but will grow in partial shade.

Propagation Divide fleshy roots in spring; pot plantlets any time.

Repotting Whenever plant is overcrowded. Best done in spring or summer.

Grooming Trim ends of leaves if they turn brown.

Pests and problems Scales may be a problem. Pale, limp, and yellowing leaves result from too much heat and too little light. Brown tips may come from salts accumulating in the potting mix from underpotting. Stems will produce no plantlets if the plant is too young or lacks light.

Chrysanthemum × morifolium

Florist's chrysanthemum, florist's mum

These greenhouse hybrids, often given as gifts, are considered houseplants because they are most often purchased to be displayed in the home while blooming. The small plants with large flowers of every color except blue are available throughout the year.

Look for plants that are near or in full bloom. Place the plant in a cool room on a windowsill where it will receive about 4 hours of direct sun daily. Morning or evening sun is best. It should bloom for 6 to 8 weeks.

Chrysanthemums do well with average to high indoor humidity levels. Do not feed when in flower, but fertilize lightly with each watering at all other times.

If you want to save the plant, prune it back and reduce watering, then plant it in your garden. Pinch back often to maintain a full, bushy plant.

Temperature 60° to 65° F days; 45° to 50° F nights.

Water Keep evenly moist. Plant tends to dry out quickly.

Light Direct sun in morning and at dusk. Bright light is essential.

Propagation Take stem tip cuttings of new shoots in spring.

Repotting Not usually done.

Grooming For sturdy plants with big flowers, pinch back frequently before buds appear. After blooming, cut stems back to 3 inches.

Pests and problems Spider mites may be a problem if plant is too dry. Leaves wilt if potting mix dries out. High temperatures cause flowers to develop rapidly and die quickly. Often buds that fail to open did not receive enough light.

Cissus

Kangaroo-ivy, kangaroo vine, oak-leaf ivy, trailing begonia, begonia-treebine, grape ivy

These vigorous, trailing evergreen vines with grapelike tendrils can grow to be 20 feet long. A better hanging plant is hard to find. *C. antarctica*, known as kangaroo-ivy or kangaroo vine because it grows by leaps and bounds, has elongated, shiny green leaves. *C. capensis*, oak-leaf ivy, has leaves shaped similarly to the oak. *C. discolor*, trailing begonia or begonia-treebine, the group's showy member, has rosy stems and green leaves flushed silver-rose but is more difficult to grow than the others. *C. rhombifolia* is the popular grape ivy, with dark green leaves formed of 3 leaflets.

Cissus can withstand neglect and poor conditions. Grow them in a hanging container or provide support for climbing and framing. The plant will grow in partial shade but prefers bright indirect light. Feed lightly with each watering throughout the growing season and provide average indoor humidity levels. Feed less if the plant is growing in low light. *C. discolor* requires more light and higher humidity than other cissus.

Temperature 65° to 75° F days; 55° to 65° F nights.

Water Water thoroughly when mix is dry an inch below the surface.

Cissus rhombifolia

Fortunella margarita 'Nagami'

Light Bright indirect light or curtain-filtered direct light. *C. rhombifolia* will survive low (reading-level) light.

Propagation Easy, from stem cuttings any time.

Repotting Repot overcrowded plants any time.

Grooming Pinch back stems to control shape.

Pests and problems Provide adequate drainage, since this plant is prone to root rot. Powdery mildew occurs occasionally. Whiteflies may be a problem on *C. discolor*.

Citrus

Citrus, calamondin orange, meyer lemon, ponderosa lemon, sweet orange, kumquat

Plants in the citrus family have something for all seasons: shiny dark green foliage; attractively scented white flowers that appear intermittently throughout the year; and colorful, long-lasting fruits that range in color from green to yellow or orange.

Growing citrus from store-bought fruit is a popular pastime. Sow the seeds in small pots in a moist growing me-dium, and cover with plastic wrap. Place the pot in a warm, brightly lit spot. The seedlings will appear in 2 to 3 weeks. Or start new plants from stem cuttings of selections that bloom well indoors.

The best choice for indoor growing is × *Citrofortunella mitis* (calamondin orange). It blooms and produces fruit the year around, and also remains nicely compact with only minimal pruning. *Citrus limon* 'Meyer' (meyer lemon) is also productive indoors. *C. limon* 'Ponderosa' (ponderosa lemon) produces enormous fruits with a thick, rough skin. *C. sinensis* cultivars (sweet oranges) require ideal conditions to produce fruit indoors. *Fortunella margarita* (kumquat) produces small, oblong orange-yellow fruits.

Citrus fruits produced indoors tend to be sour or bitter and cannot be eaten fresh. They can, however, be used in any recipe that calls for citrus, such as marmalades and candies. To ensure fruit production indoors, dust each flower with a small paintbrush, passing from flower to flower.

Citrus do well with average indoor humidity levels. Feed lightly with an acid-based fertilizer with each watering throughout the year and add trace elements once a year, in spring.

Temperature 65° to 70° F days; 50° to 55° F nights.

Water Let plant approach dryness before watering, then water thoroughly and discard drainage each time.

Light Provide 4 hours or more of direct sunlight from a south window.

Propagation Take stem cuttings in late summer.

Potting mix All-purpose or slightly acidic mix.

Repotting Repot infrequently.

Grooming Keep to desired height and shape with light pruning or clipping at any time.

Pests and problems Spider mites, mealybugs, and scales may be a problem. Will not bloom if light is too low. Leaves will drop if potting mix is too wet or too dry. Yellow leaves indicate a lack of trace elements, particularly iron.

Clivia miniata

Clivia, Kaffir-lily

This member of the amaryllis family is named after Charlotte Clive, Duchess of Northumberland, who developed it as an indoor plant. Thick stems 12 to 15 inches long emerge from a crown of leathery straplike leaves to support large clusters of trumpet-shaped orange flowers with yellow throats. French and Belgian hybrids come in yellow to deep red-orange. After flowers fade in late spring, ornamental red berries appear, providing a touch of lasting color.

This winter bloomer will do well in a room that receives plenty of indirect sunlight, has average indoor humidity levels, and also cools down overnight. Crowded roots left undisturbed for years produce the best blooms; repotting is rarely necessary. During the fall the plant rests: Apply no fertilizer and reduce water. From January to August feed once a month.

Temperature 68° to 72° F days; 50° to 55° F nights. Minimum winter temperature 45° F.

Codiaeum variegatum var. *pictum*

Coleus × *hybridus* 'Red Flash'

Clivia miniata

Water Water frequently during flowering. After flowering, allow potting mix to dry out between watering.

Light Ample bright indirect light. Curtain-filtered light is best.

Propagation In late spring divide bulbs.

Potting mix All-purpose mix or African violet mix.

Repotting Only every 3 to 4 years. If the mix level is lowered, add new mix to the top of the pot.

Grooming Pick off yellowed leaves.

Codiaeum variegatum
Croton, Joseph's coat

The varied shapes and exotic colors of the croton's leaves make it an especially attractive plant to feature in a home. Reaching up to 3 feet high, its lance-shaped, leathery leaves up to 18 inches long grow from a single stem or trunk. Foliage colors of the many different varieties include red, pink, orange, brown, and white; color markings vary considerably among in-

dividual leaves on the same plant. In addition, the plant will sometimes change colors as it matures.

C. variegatum pictum, Joseph's coat, is a popular croton featuring oval, lobed, oaklike leaves in a wide range of colors on a narrow shrub that usually attains a height of 2 to 4 feet.

Crotons are not easy to grow unless you can satisfy all their environmental needs. Lots of sunshine and a warm location free of drafts are the essentials. Keep the plant humid enough to cope with the sun and warm temperatures by placing it on a humidifying tray. Dry air or dry potting mix will cause the leaves to wither and die rapidly. Fertilize lightly with each watering throughout the growing season.

Temperature 75° to 80° F days; 65° to 70° F nights. Protect from temperatures below 60° F.

Water Keep evenly moist. Water less in winter.

Light 4 hours of direct sunlight daily. A southern or western exposure is best. Sun-

shine enhances the foliage coloring.

Propagation In summer, root stem cuttings of softwood. Air-layer any time.

Repotting In early spring, only if plant is crowded.

Grooming Clean leaves and inspect for pests regularly. Pinching or pruning will increase bushiness.

Pests and problems Highly susceptible to spider mites. Brown tips on leaves are caused by dry air or dry potting mix. Brown-edged leaves result from low temperatures.

Coleus × hybridus
Coleus

So richly colored are the leaves of this member of the mint family that many people believe coleus is the most colorful, inexpensive substitute for the croton; as a result it's been tagged the "poor man's croton." Coleus is a fast-growing tropical shrub composed of oval, scalloped leaves tapering to a point. The velvety leaves come in a multitude of colors with toothed and fringed margins, depend-

ing on the variety. Blue or white flowers form in fall.

Place coleus in a brightly lit, warm spot with average to high indoor humidity levels. Water regularly and fertilize lightly with each watering while the plant is actively growing. Nip flower buds to encourage compact growth and branching.

Temperature 75° to 80° F days; 65° to 70° F nights.

Water Keep evenly moist. Reduce water in winter. Do not use hard water.

Light Place in bright indirect light. Protect from high noon sun.

Propagation From seed, or take stem cuttings in spring or summer. Very easy to root from stem cuttings.

Repotting Repot when plant becomes pot bound.

Grooming Pinch tips of shrub to encourage bushy growth. Nip buds of flowers to retard reproductive cycle.

Pests and problems Mealybugs may be a problem. Some leaf drop in winter is normal. Leggy stems result from too little light or lack of pinching.

Columnea

Cyclamen persicum

Columnea
Columnea

There are some 150 different species of this Gesneriad family member that comes from the damp tropical forests of Central and South America and the West Indies. These semiupright or trailing plants look especially attractive in hanging containers. The brightly colored tubular flowers come in orange, scarlet, and yellow and will often bloom throughout the year in ideal conditions. Flowers range in size from ½ inch to 4 inches, depending on the variety. Leaves vary from button size to 3 inches long.

C. × banksii, which has waxy leaves and reddish orange flowers, is one of the easiest to grow. *C. gloriosa* has hairy leaves and red flowers. Also, consider investing in everblooming hybrids, such as 'Early Bird' and 'Mary Ann', which bloom more readily.

These aren't the easiest plants to grow, but keeping the air moist will help them stay healthy and blooming; use a humidifier for best results. During the winter water carefully and keep them away from heat sources. Feed lightly with each watering only when the plant is actively growing or flowering.

Temperature   70° F days; 65° F nights. Cooler in winter.

Water   Potting mix should be kept moist. Reduce water in winter.

Light   Bright indirect light.

Propagation   Take stem cuttings after flowering. Apply bottom heat.

Repotting   Repot in late spring every 2 to 3 years.

Grooming   As soon as flowering ceases, cut back stems.

Pests and problems   Subject to crown rot in overly moist conditions. Will not bloom if light is too low.

Cyclamen
Cyclamen

Heart-shaped dark green leaves surround upright stems topped with butterflylike blossoms from midautumn until midspring. *C. persicum* is most commonly grown indoors and readily available through florists. It's best to purchase your plants in early fall.

This plant prefers a cool room with average to high indoor humidity levels and good air circulation but no drafts. When blooming, it needs as much sun as possible. Feed lightly with each watering throughout the growing season.

Cyclamen can be kept after blooming if they are given special care. After blooming ceases and the foliage dies down, keep the tuber in a cool spot and let the potting mix dry out. In midsummer, repot with new potting mix in a small pot and place the plant in a warm spot to encourage good root growth. As the plant grows, gradually return it to a cool location (55° F) to induce blooming.

Temperature   60° to 65° F days; nights 60° F or lower, 40° to 50° F is ideal.

Water   Keep evenly moist but do not let plant sit in water.

Light   Bright reflected light or a curtain-filtered southern or western exposure is best.

Propagation   From seed in early spring. *C. persicum* strains bloom only after 15 to 18 months. Or divide large tubers in early fall.

Potting mix   African violet mix or 2 parts peat moss, 1 part all-purpose potting mix, and 1 part sharp sand or perlite.

Repotting   The beetlike tuber should be replanted to the same depth it had been planted previously. About half of it will show above the potting mix level. Set the pot outside and keep the mix barely moist for the remainder of the summer.

Pests and problems   Mealybugs and scales may be a problem. Moistening the depression in the center of the tuber while watering could lead to rot. Overly warm temperatures can stop flowering.

Cyperus
Umbrella plant, pygmy papyrus

The most popular indoor cyperus is *C. alternifolius*. The long green stems bear whorls of "leaves," resembling the spokes of an umbrella. These are actually bracts, among which small green to

Cyperus alternifolius

Cephalocereus senilis

Echinocactus grusonii

Cereus peruvianus

Echinopsis silvestrii

brown flowers appear. Dwarf cultivars are available. Cyperus likes wet conditions, preferring to stand in water at all times. The bracts may scorch or burn in dry indoor air. Tall plants require staking. Feed lightly with each watering while the plant is actively growing.

Temperature 60° to 65° F days; 40° to 45° F nights.

Water Keep very moist at all times. Can stand in water.

Light Keep in about 4 hours of direct sunlight in winter; provide curtain-filtered sunlight from a south- or west-facing window in summer.

Propagation Divide an old specimen or take cuttings of bract clusters.

Repotting Repot in winter or early spring, as needed.

Grooming Pick off yellowed bracts.

Pests and problems Spider mites may be a problem if air is too dry. Bracts will scorch if plant is in a draft or dry air.

Desert Cacti

The large family of cacti encompasses more than 2,000 plants, all of which are succulents. It is not true that spines are the distinguishing characteristic between cacti and other succulents. Most cacti have spines, but some do not. However, desert cacti are distinguishable from other succulents by areoles, the small sunken or raised spots on their stems from which spines, flowers, and leaves emerge and grow. There are hundreds of different kinds of cacti.

Desert cacti are extremely tolerant plants. They do need a highly porous potting mix that drains well. Although cacti prefer a relatively dry mix, they should be watered occasionally and fed with a low-nitrogen fertilizer with every watering during their growing season, usually from early spring to midautumn. Place in a sunny window with warm daytime temperatures. At night the temperature should drop 10° to 15° F. Most cacti need a cool, dry, dormant period in winter to bloom well the following spring or summer. Dry air is generally not harmful, but keep plants out of drafts.

Aporocactus flagelliformis
Rattail cactus

Rattail cactus produces narrow stems ½ inch wide and up to 6 feet long. The pink flowers are large and are borne all along the stems in summer. It has aerial roots that grip onto rock faces. For indoor culture, place the plant in a hanging container and occasionally remove the old brown stems.

Cephalocereus senilis
Oldman cactus

This upright cylindrical cactus can reach a height of 10 feet and a diameter of 8 to 10 inches. Its gray-green body develops soft, hairy spines while still immature. Funnel-shaped white or rose-colored flowers are borne on the top of the cactus after the plant is many years old and very large. The young plants in this slow-growing genus make good windowsill specimens.

Cereus
Peruvian apple, curiosity-plant

Cereus species have deeply ribbed blue-green stems. Certain cultivars, such as *C. peruvianus* 'Monstrosus', are noted for the numerous deformed growths that cover the plant. Cereus can reach a height of 20 feet. Large flowers, borne all along the stems in summer, open at night.

Echinocactus grusonii
Echinocactus, golden barrel cactus

A popular, globe-shaped cactus, golden barrel cactus has yellow spines prominently borne along its stem ribs. It grows slowly but can reach 3 feet in diameter. Bell-shaped yellow flowers are borne on the top central ring in summer. This plant will tolerate moderately lit locations but will not grow or flower in them.

Echinopsis
Urchin cactus

Globular to oval gray-green stems that grow singly or in clusters characterize the genus *Echinopsis*. The stems are distinctly ribbed, and have clusters of spines along the ribs. This cactus is best known for its large, long-lasting, funnel-shaped flowers. They range from white to yellow to pink and sometimes reach 8 inches in length. This small-

Mammillaria bocasana

Opuntia microdasys

Dieffenbachia 'Tropic Snow'

growing, free-flowering species makes a good windowsill specimen.

Gymnocalycium
Chin cactus, spider cactus

The globular stems of *Gymnocalycium* grow in clusters or singly, each stem measuring 8 to 12 inches thick, depending on the species. *G. denudatum*, also called the spider cactus, features needle-shaped yellowish spines. The bell-shaped white to pale rose flowers are borne near the top of the plant in spring and summer. *G. mihanovichii* is tiny, with pink or yellow flowers. *G.* 'Hibotan' is a bright red variety of *G. mihanovichii* that makes an unusual addition to any plant collection. This variety prefers some shade. These plants are often found grafted onto another cactus stem.

Mammillaria
Pincushion cactus, snowball cactus, little candles cactus, silver cluster cactus, rose pincushion

The numerous and extremely diverse members of the genus *Mammillaria* grow in globular to cylindrical forms. Sizes

range from tiny individual heads only a few inches wide to massive clumps. Unlike other cacti, whose flowers are borne on areoles, *Mammillaria* blooms from the joints of tubercles in a ring around the top of the plant from March to October.

M. bocasana, the snowball cactus, displays many hooked yellowish spines and bell-shaped yellow flowers. The variety *M. bocasana* 'Inermis' is spineless.

M. prolifera is a small, globe-shaped cactus with bristly white spines and yellow flowers. It is commonly called little candles cactus or silver cluster cactus.

M. zeilmanniana, the rose pincushion, is composed of a solitary stem topped with purple flowers in early summer.

Opuntia
Opuntia, bunny-ears

A growth habit of a flattened stem resembling a pad characterizes most of this species. Small tufts of spines create a dotted pattern over the surface of the plant. *O. microdasys*, called bunny-ears, has

flat pads growing out of the top of larger mature pads, creating the look that gave it its name. Bunny-ears require very little care once they are established.

Care of Desert Cacti

Temperature   To set flower buds: 60° to 65° F days; 40° to 45° F nights. At other times: 65° to 70° F days; 50° to 55° F nights.

Water   Water thoroughly when potting mix is dry an inch below the surface. During dormancy, water sparingly. Do not allow roots to stand in water; they will rot.

Light   Full sun. Ideal for a windowsill.

Propagation   Can be propagated by seed, division, or cuttings. Sow fresh seed in well-aerated potting mix and place in a warm, moist environment. You can also divide an old specimen or take cuttings.

Potting mix   Cactus mix or a very porous mix of 2 parts loam, 2 parts sand, 1 part leaf mold.

Repotting   Repot infrequently. Handle plant with extreme care. Wear leather

gloves for protection. Wrap and tape the top of the plant in newspaper before handling.

Grooming   None usually needed.

Pests and problems   Scales and mealybugs may be a problem. Root or stem rot results from poor drainage, poor air circulation, too-frequent watering, or cool, moist conditions. Will not bloom if light is too low.

Dieffenbachia
Dieffenbachia, dumb-cane

Touched to the tongue, the sap from the canelike stems of dieffenbachia can cause temporary speechlessness and much pain; hence the name "dumb-cane." The species and older hybrids of this handsome evergreen feature a single thick trunk when young; modern hybrids unwind into multiple trunks to create a palmlike appearance as the plant matures. Arching, oblong, pointed leaves 10 to 12 inches long spiral around the trunk. The leaves of some dieffenbachias are marbled or spotted. Mature plants reach a height of 6 feet and above. For

Dizygotheca elegantissima

Dracaena fragrans 'Massangeana'

planters and large container decorations, dieffenbachias have few equals.

Place in a moderately bright spot; a northern or eastern exposure is fine. Keep air moist always and feed lightly with each watering during the growing season. The sap is poisonous; avoid touching it at all times.

Temperature   75° to 80° F days; 65° to 70° F nights.

Water   When potting mix is dry to the touch, water thoroughly. Do not overwater.

Light   Moderate light; will survive low (reading-level) light.

Propagation   In spring or summer, air-layer or take root stem cuttings. Protect yourself from burning, poisonous sap.

Repotting   When crowded, repot.

Grooming   Bathe leaves occasionally and remove withered foliage promptly.

Dizygotheca elegantissima
False-aralia

This is one of the most graceful plants you can grow indoors.

Thin dark green leaves with lighter veins spread fingerlike into 9 segments with sawtoothed edges. You can buy thumb-pot seedlings for terrariums, or a mature plant large enough to sit under.

With the right care, this slow grower should cause few problems. It's extremely sensitive to the level of moisture in the potting mix: Soggy mix is unacceptable, yet a dry rootball will cause the leaves to yellow. Also, this plant does not like being moved around. Feed lightly with each watering while the plant is actively growing and provide moist air at all times.

Temperature   68° to 75° F days; 65° to 70° F nights.

Water   Keep evenly moist from April to October. Reduce water in winter.

Light   Bright indirect light. Older plants can endure less light.

Propagation   Difficult; not recommended for home gardeners.

Repotting   In spring every 2 years. Prefers to be pot bound.

Grooming   Keep to desired height and shape with light pruning or clipping at any time.

Pests and problems   Spider mites may be a problem. Lower leaf drop may result from exposure to drafts or incorrect watering, although these plants also lose their lower leaves as they get older.

Dracaena
Cornplant, golddust dracaena, Madagascar dragontree, red-margined dracaena, pleomele

These palmlike members of the Lily family feature a single stem with a tuft of swordlike leaves on top. When mature, the tree can reach a height of 10 feet or more.

Many different dracaena varieties are available. Plain green *D. fragrans* 'Massangeana' (cornplant) occasionally yields sprays of fragrant white flowers among its large leaves. *D. surculosa*, formerly called *D. godseffiana* and known as the golddust dracaena, has narrow stems and broad leaves marbled with white and gold, and is miniature in comparison to the others. *D.*

marginata (Madagascar dragontree, red-margined dracaena) has thin red-edged leaves atop trunks that naturally zigzag and curve.

D. deremensis grows as a single-stemmed plant with long, narrow leaves arching outward all along the stem. *D. deremensis* 'Janet Craig' has shiny dark green leaves and will grow to 5 to 6 feet if given ample light. A dwarf cultivar, *D. deremensis* 'Janet Craig Compacta', is also available. 'Warneckii' has narrower leaves with thin long stripes along the leaf edges.

D. reflexa (pleomele), formerly sold as *Pleomele reflexa*, grows into a large plant with reflexed, or downward-pointing, leaves set closely along canelike stems. The best known of the variegated cultivars is 'Song of India', with white- or cream-edged leaves.

Dracaenas can endure shade and low winter temperatures. In general, warmth and abundant light are the keys to strong growth. Feed lightly with each watering throughout the growing season. In spring or summer,

Dracaena deremensis 'Warneckii'

Epipremnum aureum

stimulate new growth and re-juvenate old plants by cutting back 6 to 8 inches.

Temperature   75° to 80° F days; 65° to 70° F nights.

Water   Keep potting mix barely moist, but not soggy, at all times.

Light   Bright indirect light or curtain-filtered direct sunlight.

Propagation   Take suckers from plant base, 3-inch stem cuttings from young plants, or air-layer older plants.

Repotting   Repot infrequently.

Grooming   Periodically wipe dust and grime from leaves. Pick off yellowed leaves. Trim brown leaf tips.

Pests and problems   Brown tips and yellow edges on leaves are caused by dry air, underwatering, or cold drafts. Surround pot with moist peat. Brown spots on leaves result from dryness at the roots. Pale leaves that curve downward with brown edges result from low temperatures. Yellowing or loss of lower leaves is natural in older leaves.

Epipremnum aureum

Epipremnum, pothos; devil's-ivy

Pothos is also known as *Scindapsus aureus*. Sometimes mistaken for a philodendron, this versatile climbing plant will grow in water for months, keep in a planter for years, or frame a window. Pothos feature heart-shaped apple green leaves boldly splashed with creamy yellow. *E. aureum* 'Marble Queen' is heavily marbled with pure white.

Pothos is very hardy. Keep the plant out of drafts in a warm, well-lit location with average humidity levels. Let potting mix dry to the touch between waterings and fertilize lightly with each watering while the plant is actively growing.

Temperature   65° to 70° F days; 50° to 60° F nights. Cooler in winter.

Water   Water frequently during the spring and summer, less in winter.

Light   Moderate or bright indirect light.

Propagation   Take stem cuttings in spring. Keep mix barely moist and place in dark until rooted.

Repotting   In spring, when necessary.

Grooming   Pinch growth tips to induce bushiness.

Pests and problems   Lack of variegation results from poor light.

Episcia

Flame-violet

This relative of the African violet makes a striking hanging plant with its runners, or stolons, which cascade down the sides of the pot. *E. cupreata* (flame-violet) has small, tubular reddish orange flowers among erect leaves that are copper colored with silver veins. Hybrids allow for various foliage and flower colors. These summer bloomers make attractive foliage plants the rest of the year.

Episcias need lots of moisture in the air. To provide the needed moisture, surround the base of the plant with damp peat. Runners will root easily in the surrounding mix to form plantlets. Feed lightly with each watering only when the plant is actively growing or flowering.

Temperature   Average warmth: 75° F days; 65° to 70° F nights. Not less than 55° F in winter.

Water   Keep evenly moist at all times during growing season. Reduce amount of water in winter.

Light   No direct sun, just bright light. Plants need at least 14 to 16 hours of bright indirect light or artificial light a day.

Propagation   Layer runners in compost; they will root and form plantlets. You can also root stem and leaf cuttings and side shoots.

Potting mix   African violet mix or 2 parts peat moss, 1 part all-purpose potting mix, and 1 part sharp sand or perlite.

Repotting   Every spring.

Grooming   Pinch off tips of stems to encourage branching. For fresh growth, cut back plant when it has stopped blooming. To increase blooming, remove some of the stolons.

Episcia 'Teddy Bear'

Euphorbia pulcherrima

Exacum affine

Fatsia japonica

Pests and problems Brown leaf tips are the result of dry air.

Euphorbia pulcherrima
Poinsettia

The poinsettia was first found in the 1800s growing as a wild-flower in Mexico, and since has been cultivated in the United States to become the most popular live Christmas gift given today. The large white, yellow, pink, or red flower is actually a group of bracts that surround a small, inconspicuous true flower. Ranging in height from 1 to 3 feet, some plants have blossoms that stretch 6 to 12 inches across.

With proper care these plants will continue to bloom for several months and some can be made to blossom the following season. While blooming the plants simply need plenty of sun, average indoor humidity levels, and protection from drafts and sudden changes in temperature. Reduce water during the rest period from spring to mid-summer, then increase

waterings and feed lightly with each watering. Beginning about October 1, these plants need several weeks of long (12-hour) nights, uninterrupted by any light source, before flowers are initiated. If your plant is indoors, be sure that household lights do not interrupt this darkness requirement. Once the bracts begin to show color, the plant can be given regular indoor growing conditions.

Temperature 68° F or above days; 50° to 65° F nights.

Water Allow potting mix to dry somewhat, then water thoroughly. Reduce water during rest period.

Light A sunny western or southern exposure is best. In summer this location may become too hot; if so, move the plant farther from the window or protect it with curtains during the heat of the day.

Propagation Root cuttings of tips of new growth in summer.

Potting mix Slightly acidic mix.

Repotting Repot infrequently in winter or early spring, as needed.

Grooming Thin out branches in summer to produce larger bracts. Pinching back will make the plant bushier but also may reduce the size of the bracts.

Pests and problems White-flies may be a problem. Leaves will drop if potting mix is too wet or too dry, or if plant is suddenly moved to a spot where light is too low.

Exacum affine
Persian violet

Persian violets are popular because they will bloom in small pots. Plants are commonly covered with tiny blue or white flowers with yellow centers and are available in a variety of sizes. Provide direct sun in fall to encourage blooming. Persian violets require moist air; use a humidifier for best results. Feed lightly with each watering while the plant is growing or flowering.

Temperature 70° to 75° F days; 55° to 60° F nights.

Water Keep evenly moist.

Light Keep in about 4 hours of direct sunlight in winter. Provide curtain-filtered sun-

light from a south or west window in summer.

Propagation Start from seed in spring. Cuttings do not produce as fine a plant.

Potting mix African violet mix.

Repotting Transplant seedlings several times as they grow.

Grooming Discard after flowering.

Pests and problems White-flies may be a problem. Dry potting mix or a high level of soluble salts may cause plant to die back. Crown rot results from overly moist conditions.

× Fatshedera lizei

See *Fatsia*

Fatsia japonica
Japanese aralia, aralia-ivy, tree-ivy

This handsome evergreen foliage plant has bold, lobed leaves of shiny green, occasionally variegated with white. In frost-free climates it can be grown outdoors, but it also makes an excellent contribution to indoor gardens.

Fern: Nephrolepis exaltata 'Bostoniensis'

Fern: Asplenium nidus

Fern: Davallia mariesii

The smaller plant, × *Fatshedera lizei* (aralia-ivy or tree-ivy), is a hybrid of *Fatsia* and English ivy; it has *Fatsia*'s leaves and the growth habit of ivy.

Being both durable and tolerant, Japanese aralia is a fast and easy grower. Place it in a cool, well-ventilated location with bright light and average humidity levels. Wash and mist the leaves regularly and feed lightly with every watering during the growing season. Move the plant to a cool, dry spot during winter. Remove any flower buds that may emerge in the mature plant to prevent it from entering the reproductive cycle.

Temperature   65° to 70° F days; 60° to 65° F nights. No warmer than 70° F in winter.

Water   Keep potting mix evenly moist during growing season. Water sparingly in winter.

Light   Moderate or bright indirect light.

Propagation   In summer take stem cuttings.

Repotting   Prefers to be pot bound. Repot when roots fill pot.

Grooming   Clean foliage regularly. Be careful not to bruise tender leaves. Trim back severely if plant becomes gangly.

Ferns

Although ferns lack flowers, the delicate composition of their fronds instills a room with a peaceful calm that a flower may have trouble duplicating. This refined plant is probably the oldest houseplant on the evolutionary time line; only the algae and the mosses come earlier.

The secret to successfully growing ferns lies in your ability to match the moist, cool air and light shade of the tropical forest that is their natural growing environment as nearly as possible. Since their natural home is in dappled brightness, avoid exposing them to direct sunlight. Hot, dry air spells real trouble to ferns. The air as well as the potting mix must always be kept moist. Provide humidity by placing the pot on a humidifying tray or in a larger pot of moist peat moss. Most ferns will grow well in average

temperatures during the day with a drop at night.

Fertilize most ferns lightly once a year in early spring. Fertilize Boston ferns lightly with each watering throughout the year.

Adiantum
Maidenhair fern

With their slender black stems and delicate fronds lined with broad, frilled leaflets, maidenhair ferns are especially attractive in groupings. They require ample light and humidity in order to survive indoors and do well in terrariums.

Asplenium nidus
Bird's-nest fern, spleenwort

The graceful, wavy, lance-shaped bright green fronds of the bird's-nest fern grow to be 3 feet long. They emerge from a dark crown that resembles a bird's nest.

Davallia
Squirrel's-foot fern, deer's-foot fern, rabbit's-foot fern

The squirrel's-foot-fern features wiry, 10-inch stems of small fronds with leaflets. Its curious furry rhizomes give it its common names. It is an

excellent choice for a hanging container.

Nephrolepis exaltata
Boston fern

One of the most popular indoor plants, *Nephrolepis* are perfect in pots or hanging containers. The long, swordlike fronds of this plant stand erect and can grow up to 3 feet in length. There are several varieties: *N. exaltata* 'Bostoniensis', the Boston fern, arches more than most, so it looks especially good in a hanging container. 'Fluffy Ruffles' has ruffled leaf edges; 'Whitmannii' has lacy leaf edges.

Pellaea rotundifolia
Button fern

This small fern derives its common name from its round, leathery leaflets that look like buttons. The frond's growth pattern is more horizontal than erect.

Platycerium bifurcatum
Staghorn fern

The staghorn fern grows best attached to pieces of bark or other porous material because it's an epiphyte, or air plant. The broad, lancelike fronds

Fern: Adiantum

Fern: Platycerium bifurcatum

Ficus benjamina

Ficus lyrata

Fern: Pellaea rotundifolia

Fern: Pteris cretica

Ficus pumila

Ficus deltoidea

divide about in the middle of their 2-foot length and the ends take on the appearance of stag antlers. Never allow this plant to dry out.

Polypodium aureum

Bear's-paw fern, hare's-foot fern, golden polypody fern

This tolerant, low-growing fern has scaly, creeping rusty brown rhizomes, wiry stems, and bold, straplike, leathery leaves. *P. aureum,* the hare's-foot fern, consists of many deeply cut ruffled leaflets and fronds that can grow 2 to 5 feet long. The fronds of *P. aureum* 'Mandaianum' are blue-green above and whitish beneath. This plant does well in a hanging container.

Pteris cretica

Table fern

Long, straplike leaves divide at the tips of this fern. Some forms are variegated, with narrow or crested leaves. *P. cretica* 'Wimsettii' is light green in color, and the mature form has forked leaf tips that become dense and frilly. *P. cretica albo-lineata* (variegated table fern) has slightly wavy leaflets with a broad

band of creamy white down the center of each. These ferns look best when displayed in dish gardens or small pots.

Care of Ferns

Temperature   Average: 60° to 70° F days; cooler nights. Minimum temperature of 50° to 55° F.

Water   Mix must be kept moist but not wet. Never allow plant to dry out. Reduce watering during winter.

Light   Bright indirect light. An east or north window is ideal, but almost any location protected from direct sun will do.

Propagation   It's easiest to divide large clumps or detach offsets and cultivate. Spores may also be collected from the underside of fronds.

Repotting   Necessary once a year before the growing season. If roots do not fill the pot and repotting is unnecessary, simply remove 1 to 2 inches of potting mix and add fresh mix.

Grooming   Remove old or discolored fronds promptly. Remove any moss that grows

on pot or mix surface and loosen topsoil.

Pests and problems   Aphids, mealybugs, spider mites, and thrips may be a problem. Brown tips on leaves result from dry air.

Ficus

Ficus, fig, ornamental fig tree, weeping fig, mistletoe fig, rubber plant, fiddleleaf fig, creeping fig, variegated rooting fig

This large, diverse family of more than 800 tropical trees and shrubs includes not only the edible fig, *Ficus carica,* but a number of ornamental plants perfect for container gardening. Provided with good light, rich, evenly moist potting mix, and frequent light feeding, ficus will grow well. Guard against overwatering, and protect from cold drafts, dry heat, and sudden changes in environment. If moved to a new location, often the plant will lose most of its leaves as it adjusts. With care it will flourish again.

F. benjamina, the weeping fig, holds a prominent position in the container plant world. The bark is birchlike, with

graceful, arching branches loaded with glossy, pointed leaves. It grows from 2 to 18 feet tall. *F. nitida* is a name often given to more upright versions of *F. benjamina*. It may also refer to a similar species, *F. microcarpa.*

F. deltoidea, the mistletoe fig (formerly known as *F. diversifolia*), bears spreading branches covered with small, round to wedge-shaped leaves and many tiny (but inedible) green figs that turn red in bright sun.

F. elastica and the larger-leaved *F. elastica* 'Decora' are old favorites commonly referred to as rubber plants. They have bold deep green leaves on stems from 2 to 10 feet tall. *F. elastica* 'Variegata' has long, narrow leaves that make a rippling pattern of grass green, metallic gray, and creamy yellow. When a rubber plant becomes too lanky, cut off the top and select a side branch to form a new main shoot, or air-layer the plant.

F. lyrata (also known as *F. pandurata*) is the fiddleleaf fig, a striking container plant. It has durable, leathery leaves

Fittonia verschaffeltii var. *argyroneura*

Hedera helix 'Kolibri'

of deep green in a fiddle shape. The plant can grow from 5 to 10 feet tall.

F. pumila, the creeping fig, has tiny, heart-shaped leaves. This fast-growing trailer is a good plant for hanging containers or a cascading shelf plant.

F. sagittata 'Variegata', the variegated rooting fig, also sold as *F. radicans,* bears thin, pointed, 2- to 4-inch leaves heavily marked with creamy white. It makes an elegant hanging container plant. Brown patches in the variegated areas are due to too much cold or sun.

F. maclellandii 'Alii' is a recent introduction, with long, narrow, pointed leaves that give it a bamboolike appearance. It is more tolerant of being moved than *F. benjamina.*

Temperature   75° to 85° F days; 60° to 65° F nights.

Water   Water thoroughly when potting mix is dry 2 inches below the mix surface. Reduce amount in winter.

Light   Bright light. An eastern or western exposure is best.

Propagation   By air layering or stem cuttings.

Potting mix   All-purpose mix. *F. pumila* and *F. sagittata* like a richer mix and more moisture and shade than the other ficus.

Repotting   Prefers to be pot bound. Repot every 3 to 4 years in spring until plant is preferred size or too large to handle.

Grooming   Clean leaves occasionally.

Pests and problems   Check regularly for pests or fungus disease. Yellowing leaf edges and some loss of lower foliage result from underfeeding or are signs of an insect or fungus problem. Dry, shriveled leaves in trailing types is caused by too much direct sun.

Fittonia
Fittonia, nerve-plant, mosaic-plant

The intricately veined, oval leaves of the nerve plant grow semiupright and trail over the sides of their container. *F. verschaffeltii* var. *argyroneura* displays a mosaic pattern of white veins; another

variety, *F. verschaffeltii* var. *verschaffeltii,* has intense red veins against paper-thin olive green leaves.

Place fittonia in a warm spot that receives some light. A northern or eastern exposure is fine. Let it dry out between waterings and place on a humidifying tray to provide ample moisture in the air. Feed lightly with each watering during the growing season. During the winter move to a cool spot and water lightly.

Temperature   70° to 80° F days; 60° to 70° F nights.

Water   When potting mix is dry, water moderately.

Light   Moderate light. A north- or east-facing window is best.

Propagation   In spring, take stem cuttings.

Potting mix   African violet mix.

Repotting   Every 2 to 3 years in spring.

Grooming   Pinch and prune regularly to encourage bushiness.

Hedera helix
English ivy

Many plants are called ivy, but the most famous is *Hedera helix.* Countless varieties of this perfect trailing and climbing plant are available: 'Merion Beauty' has small leaves in the typical English ivy shape. 'Itsy Bitsy' is a tiny variety. Some, such as 'Curlilocks', have leaves that are curled, waved, or crinkled. Others have color variegation; for example, the yellow-gold and green 'California Gold' and the white 'Glacier'. Many will send out aerial roots and climb rough surfaces, such as a brick fireplace wall, or you can use them in large planters as a ground cover. They can also be trained on espaliers.

Protected from hot, dry air, English ivy will flourish as long as a few basics are followed. Place it in a cool, bright spot and keep the potting mix and air moist. During the growing season feed lightly with every watering. Bathe the foliage occasionally. Plants rest in both fall and winter.

Temperature   60° to 70° F days; 50° to 60° F nights.

Hippeastrum

Hoya carnosa 'Krinkle'

Water Keep mix evenly moist but not soggy. Provide less water during the fall and winter.

Light Bright indirect light.

Propagation By division, layering, or stem cuttings.

Repotting Every 2 to 3 years when roots become pot bound.

Grooming In spring, prune back to encourage bushiness.

Pests and problems Sparse, spindly growth and dry, brittle leaves come from hot temperatures and dry air or spider mites. Small leaves and too much stem indicate lack of light. Brown leaf tips result from dry air. Green leaves on variegated types result from too little light.

Hippeastrum
Amaryllis, Barbados lily

The strap-shaped leaves of this lilylike flower emerge after the plant blooms. Stems 1 to 2 feet long sport clusters of 3 or 4 flowers that are 8 to 10 inches across. They come in a wide array of colors. Seed-grown bulbs are sold by color in stores. Named strains available through mail-order firms tend to produce more robust flowers.

The plant blooms in late winter and is moderately easy to grow; with proper care it can last for many years. Pot prepared bulbs as early as October. When the flower spike appears, place the plant in a well-lit, cool (60° F) location. As buds grow and eventually flower, keep moist. Feed lightly with each watering when plant is actively growing or flowering. After flowering, continue feeding and watering until the foliage dies back, then allow the plant to dry up and become dormant. The plant requires average to high indoor humidity levels.

Temperature 65° to 70° F days; 60° to 65° F nights. Keep plants cooler while they are blooming.

Water Keep evenly moist while flowering.

Light Bright light. A southern or eastern exposure is best.

Propagation Small offset bulbs develop alongside the large ones. These can be planted after the main bulb is through flowering. It takes seeds 3 to 4 years to produce flowering plants.

Repotting Every 3 to 4 years. Place the bulb in a pot with a diameter that allows a 2-inch ring of potting mix around the bulb. Water well once, then wait for plant to emerge before watering again.

Grooming After flowering, do not remove foliage from the bulb until it has died back.

Hoya
Hoya, waxplant, miniature waxplant

Hoya are vining plants with thickened leaves produced on self-branching stems. Given enough light, they will produce clusters of extremely fragrant, waxy flowers in summer or fall. The flowers form on the same spurs year after year, so be careful not to prune off these leafless vine extensions. Train the plants on a trellis or use them in a hanging container; double-back the vines to give the plant a denser appearance. Many forms have variegated or variously colored leaves. *H. carnosa* (waxplant) has oval leaves that reach 3 inches long and fragrant white flowers with a reddish center. *H. bella* (miniature waxplant) has smaller, lance-shaped dull green leaves and fragrant white flowers with a red center. Keep hoyas at average indoor humidity levels and feed lightly with each watering only when the plant is actively growing or flowering.

Temperature 60° to 65° F days; 50° to 55° F nights.

Water Keep very moist during growth and flowering; at other times, allow to dry between waterings.

Light Place in a bright, indirectly lit south, east, or west window.

Propagation Take stem cuttings at any time.

Repotting Repot infrequently. New plants need to grow in a medium-to-large pot until almost root bound before they will bloom.

Grooming Keep to desired height and shape with light pruning or clipping at any time, being careful not to cut off the flower spurs.

Pests and problems Will not bloom if light is too low.

Hypoestes phyllostachya

Maranta leuconeura var.
erythroneura

Monstera deliciosa

Orchid: Cattleya

Hypoestes phyllostachya

Hypoestes, pink-polka-dot,
freckle-face

The common names for
Hypoestes come from the unusual pink spots on its leaves
(its botanical name formerly
was *H. sanguinolenta*). This
bushy plant grows rapidly in
good light, and many colorful
hybrids are now available,
including 'Pink Splash' and
red- or white-spotted cultivars.
Prune it frequently to keep it
to about 12 inches in height
and prevent legginess. It likes
moist air; use a humidifier for
best results. Feed lightly with
each watering throughout the
growing season.

Temperature   75° to 80° F
days; 65° to 70° F nights.

Water   Let plant dry out
slightly, then water thoroughly and discard drainage.

Light   Provide at least 4
hours of curtain-filtered sunlight from a bright south, east,
or west window.

Propagation   Grows easily
from seed. Take stem cuttings
at any time.

Repotting   Repot in winter
or early spring, as needed.

Grooming   Keep to desired
height and shape with light
pruning or clipping at any
time.

Pests and problems   Will
get spindly and weak if light is
too low.

Maranta leuconeura
Prayer-plant

The name "prayer-plant" refers to the growth habit of this
plant. In the daytime its sat-
iny bronze-marked foliage lays
flat; at night these leaves turn
upward, giving the appearance
of praying hands. The plant
reaches a height of about 8
inches. There are many varieties; all bear spectacular foliage with colored veins and
brush strokes of color on back-
grounds of white to black.

Although the prayer-plant
is fairly easy to grow, some of
the less common types are better left for the experienced
gardener. These plants like a
warm, humid environment in
partial shade. Direct sunlight
will cause the leaves to fade.
Surround pots with peat moss
or plant in a grouping to provide the needed humidity. The

potting mix should be moist at
all times. Feed lightly with
each watering.

Temperature   70° to 80° F
days; 60° to 70° F nights. Minimum temperature 55° F in
winter, through March. Guard
against sudden fluctuations in
temperature.

Water   Keep very moist but
not soggy during the growing
season. Barely water in
winter.

Light   Moderate light; partial
shade is best.

Propagation   By layering,
division, or stem cuttings.

Repotting   Grows best when
pot bound. Repot every 2 to 3
years in spring.

Grooming   Wash leaves and
remove withered foliage
promptly.

Pests and problems   Spider
mites may be a problem. Dry
brown-tipped leaves result
from dry air. Yellow lower
leaves and curled and spotted
upper leaves are caused by
underwatering. Limp rotting
leaves in winter come from
cold, wet environment.

Monstera deliciosa
Monstera; split-leaf
philodendron

Found in many homes, *M.
deliciosa* climbs and sends out
aerial roots that attach to supports or grow to the ground.
Stems can reach a length of 6
feet or more and sport large
perforated and deeply cut
leaves.

These plants are easy to
grow as long as you provide a
few essentials. Direct the aerial roots into the potting mix
to give support to the weak
stem, and grow under average
to high indoor humidity and
light levels. Keep the potting
mix barely moist in winter.
Feed lightly with each watering during the growing season.

Temperature   65° to 75° F
days; 65° to 70° F nights. Not
less than 50° F in winter.

Water   Water when mix is
dry to the touch. Do not waterlog. Reduce amount in winter.

Light   Bright indirect light;
will tolerate shade but will
eventually lose its charm.

Propagation   When plant
grows too tall, take stem cuttings from the top, or air-layer.

Orchid: Dendrobium

Orchid: Oncidium

Orchid: Paphiopedilum

Repotting Prefers to be pot bound. Repot every 2 to 3 years in spring.

Grooming Wash mature leaves. Guide aerial roots into potting mix for support. Cut tops of tall plants to limit growth.

Pests and problems Waterlogged potting mix will cause leaves to weep around edges. Leaves with brittle brown edges result from dry air. Brown edges and yellowed leaves are a symptom of overwatering or, less frequently, underfeeding. Dropping of lower leaves is normal.

Serious leaf drop results from moving the plant or an abrupt change in the environment. Young leaves often have no perforations. Low light also will cause small, unperforated leaves.

Orchids

Growing these exquisite, colorful flowers is regarded by most people as the supreme gardening achievement, which only experts attempt. But, in fact, some species of orchids grow quite well indoors and require less routine care than other houseplants. In addition, improved breeding techniques have significantly increased the availability and lowered the cost of many species.

Although orchids have striking flowers, their foliage is often unattractive. Many have wrinkly, lumpy pseudobulbs at the base of the leaves and bear thick, aerial roots. Many people prefer to grow orchids in an out-of-the-way spot, moving them to a more visible spot when they bloom.

It is wise to purchase mature, blooming orchids, since young plants can take years to flower. Described here are some of the orchids that grow well under average indoor conditions.

Cattleya

This large classical orchid, most often seen in corsages, is good for beginners to try. The vigorous plants produce gorgeous blooms when they receive plenty of sun. A range of miniature hybrids with smaller blooms is increasingly popular.

Cymbidium

The miniature cymbidium is especially suited for indoor gardens, but be aware that its narrow, arching foliage needs room. Flowering, which requires cool nights, usually occurs in late summer or fall. The flowers are long lasting.

Dendrobium

Dendrobiums are mostly epiphytic orchids, with both evergreen and deciduous types available. Large flowers bloom in clusters or in a row along the stem. They last for at least a week and up to several months depending on the species. These plants need plenty of sun.

Miltonia

Pansy orchid

The flat-faced, heavily marbled flowers of the pansy orchid give it its common name. The original genus has been divided into two closely related ones: *Miltonia*, with two-leaved pseudobulbs and preferring higher temperatures, and *Miltoniopsis*, with one-leaved pseudobulbs and preferring cooler temperatures. Both require filtered light and high humidity.

Oncidium

Dancing-lady

This large group of epiphytic orchids, known as dancing-lady orchids, generally produce stalks of yellow flowers speckled with brown. Flower size depends on the species. They require bright light but protection from direct summer sunlight.

Paphiopedilum

Lady's-slipper

Paphiopedilum, the lady's-slipper orchid, produces long-lasting flowers of fragrant blooms throughout the year if given plenty of moisture and a less airy potting mix than other orchids (achieved by adding extra sphagnum moss to the mix). It prefers filtered light.

Phalaenopsis

Moth-orchid

Phalaenopsis, commonly known as the moth-orchid, unfurls sprays of 2- to 3-inch flowers in a range of colors. The plant grows up to 30 inches high. This shade-loving

Orchid: Phalaenopsis

Palm: Caryota mitis

plant is easy to grow at temperatures of 75° F during the day and 60° F at night. It has attractive marbled foliage.

Care of Orchids

Orchids are an extremely varied group of plants, and their cultural requirements also vary considerably. Although this makes it difficult to give a general summary of orchid care, it also means that there is just the plant for every indoor situation.

Provide plenty of moisture in the air. Place orchids on humidifying trays. Good air circulation is a must. Feed lightly with each watering throughout the year, more heavily in summer.

Temperature Normal daytime temperatures of 70° to 75° F are fine. A nighttime temperature 15° F lower is appreciated. An annual period of cool temperatures (down to 50° F) will induce flowering in many orchids.

Water Varieties with thick leaves and large pseudobulbs prefer to be watered thoroughly, then allowed to dry out before the next watering. Those with thin roots and no

pseudobulbs generally prefer to be watered as soon as the potting mix starts to dry. Most orchids appreciate a short period of dry conditions in autumn to stimulate flowering.

Light Orchids requiring direct sunlight should be given full sun throughout the winter months, preferably in a south-facing window, and bright light with some shading from direct midday sun in summer. If they take on a yellowish tinge, all is well; if their foliage is bright green, they may need more light. This group may need supplemental artificial light during the winter. Orchids that prefer filtered light do best in either east- or west-facing windows or curtain-filtered south-facing windows the year around. They also do well under fluorescent lights.

Propagation Most orchids can be divided every few years; at least three pseudobulbs should be left in each pot. Some orchids also produce *keikis*, or plantlets, at the bases or on the flower stalks. Pot these once they have produced roots. Stake new plants.

Potting mix Use commercially prepared orchid mixture or the mix on page 22. Epiphytic orchids can also be grown in pots of osmunda fiber or ground bark.

Repotting Allow roots to extend beyond the pot as long as the plant grows well. Repot when growth is inhibited.

Grooming Pick off yellowed leaves and cut back flower stalks to the nearest green joint after blooming.

Pest and problems Limp leaves or flowers are caused first by insufficient light, second by improper watering, usually overwatering. Expect yellowing leaves if leaves are old or the plant is deciduous; otherwise, they result from overwatering or sunburn. Brown spots are caused by too much sun or leaf spot disease.

Palms

These consistently popular houseplants have graceful fans and a rich green color that can instill even the coldest northern home with a tropical flair and elegance.

This is a large and varied plant family of which only a few are grown indoors. Although they are some of the most expensive plants you can buy, they are well worth the investment. As tolerant plants, they adapt well to the limited light and controlled temperatures and humidity levels of homes. You can save money by purchasing small young plants that will slowly grow to a mature size. Some types will flourish in the home for decades.

Most palms are easy to care for and prefer similar growing conditions. During the spring and summer growing seasons, water plants heavily and feed lightly with each watering. Reduce water and stop feeding in winter. Protect from dry air and direct sunlight, especially if you move your palm outdoors. Do not prune palm trees unless an old stem or trunk dies naturally. Unlike most plants, the life-support systems of palms are located directly in the tip of the stalk. Pinching out this tip or cutting off the newest frond below its point of attachment to the trunk will eliminate all new growth.

Palm: Chrysalidocarpus lutescens

Palm: Chamaedorea elegans

Palm: Phoenix roebelenii

Palm: Howea forsterana

Palm: Rhapis

Caryota

Fishtail palm

This large palm features a thick trunk and many spreading branches, each laden with fans of dark green leaves. The ribbed texture of the leaves and the wedge shape evoke the palm's common name.

Chamaedorea elegans

Parlor palm, bamboo palm, reed palm

This palm, also known as *Neanthe bella*, features handsome light green fronds. Sometimes it bears bunches of small yellow flowers near the base of the trunk. It is a relatively small palm, growing to a height of 6 feet only after many years—perfect for entryways, living rooms, or shady decks. It can tolerate low light levels and is also useful as a terrarium plant when young.

Chrysalidocarpus lutescens

Areca palm, butterfly palm

This medium-sized, slow-growing palm features a cluster of thin, canelike stems with arching fronds and strap-shaped, shiny green leaflets.

It is extremely susceptible to spider mites.

Howea forsterana

Kentia palm

This popular palm grows to be a very large tree outdoors in nature. Indoors, *Howea* will rarely pass 7 to 8 feet. Feather-shaped leaves arch outward from sturdy stalks to create a full appearance. It will do well in low light indoors.

Phoenix roebelenii

Pygmy date palm

This date palm is a dwarf palm, growing to a height of 4 feet. A more delicate-looking palm than most, it has a straight, symmetrical shape that is composed of branching, narrow-leaved fronds with a pendulous habit.

Rhapis excelsa

Lady palm

The lady palm features 6- to 12-inch-wide fans composed of 4 to 10 thick, shiny leaves. The leaves occur at the ends of thin, arching leafstalks along a hairy brown main trunk.

This plant can reach 12 feet in height and will tolerate low light and low humidity levels.

Care of Palms

Temperature 60° to 70° F days and nights. Cooler in winter, but not less than 50° F.

Water Water liberally in spring and summer. Good drainage is important.

Light Bright light but will grow in shade.

Propagation From seed, but it's difficult.

Potting mix All-purpose mix or 1 part all-purpose mix and 1 part peat moss.

Repotting Not necessary very often. Repot in late spring or early summer.

Grooming Wash leaves to control spider mites and sucking insects. Slice off old bases of leaves at the very bottom of the trunk, taking care not to cut into the trunk.

Pests and problems Spider mites may be a problem if air is too dry. Some pesticides are harmful to palms, so check the labels carefully before using them.

Pelargonium

Geranium, florist's geranium, Martha Washington geranium, regal geranium, ivy geranium

These natives of South Africa are versatile and appealing. There are thousands of species and named varieties, and many easily move indoors from outside. They provide the most flowers in the summer months.

Common geraniums are hybrids of *Pelargonium* × *hortorum*, and often have a darker green or blackish ring on each leaf. Varieties are available in red, salmon, apricot, tangerine, pink, and white. They bloom all year, but they are most appreciated in January and February. Many become quite large, but there are also miniature and dwarf varieties available that never grow above 8 inches.

Fancy-leaf geraniums have varicolored leaves, often in shades of bronze, scarlet, and yellow. *P.* × *domesticum* (Martha Washington or regal geranium) grows to about 2½ feet. Its large flowers come in a wide range of striking colors, with some brilliantly blotched. Leaves are dark green with

Pelargonium peltatum 'Galilee'

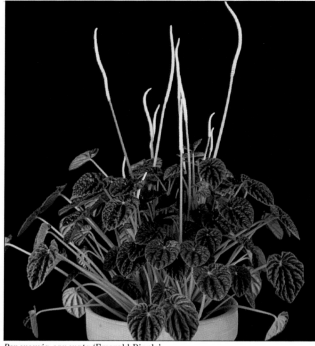

Peperomia caperata 'Emerald Ripple'

crinkled margins. It is not as popular as others because it requires cooler temperatures.

Scented-leaf varieties are grown primarily for the sharp, evocative fragrance of their leaves. Scented-leaf plants are generally smaller and more sensitive to care requirements than their cousins.

Ivy geraniums, varieties of *P. peltatum*, bear leathery leaves with a shape similar to English ivy, and sport many clusters of showy flowers, often veined with a darker shade of the overall color. These are excellent in hanging containers near windows.

Geraniums are easy to care for in the proper environment. A sunny windowsill where it is cool (never rising above 75° F), with average indoor humidity levels, is ideal. Feed lightly with each watering while the plant is actively growing or flowering.

Temperature   70° to 75° F days; nights cooler. Not less than 45° F in winter.

Water   Water thoroughly when potting mix is dry below the surface. Do not overwater, especially during the winter when less is needed.

Light   Direct sunlight for 4 hours a day is essential. Scented geraniums need less light.

Propagation   Root stem cuttings, uncovered, in moist vermiculite. You can also start many cultivars from seed.

Repotting   Repot in winter or early spring, as needed. Transplant seedlings several times as they grow.

Grooming   Pinch back in spring for bushiness. Remove flowers as they fade.

Pests and problems   White-flies may be a problem.

Peperomia

Peperomia, watermelon begonia, silverleaf peperomia, false-philodendron, creeping-buttons, baby rubber plant

Peperomia offers an astonishing variety of leaf forms, colors, and growth habits. Most are easy-to-grow, small plants, ideally suited for windowsills. Peperomias require moist air; use a humidifier for best results. Feed lightly with every watering while the plant is actively growing.

Clumping *Peperomias*

Clumping peperomias are a mass of leaves on short stems originating from a single base. *P. argyreia*, formerly known as *P. sandersii* (watermelon begonia), has thick, smooth, almost round leaves striped with green and silver. *P. caperata* 'Emerald Ripple' has small, dark, heart-shaped leaves with a deeply corrugated surface. *P. griseoargentea* (silverleaf peperomia) has a similarly corrugated surface but is silvery gray throughout. Clumping peperomias are more susceptible to crown rot than other peperomias.

Trailing *Peperomias*

Trailing peperomias have weak, pendant stems. The best known is *P. scandens* 'Variegata' (false-philodendron), which bears 2-inch, heart-shaped leaves with a broad cream edge on arching stems. *P. rotundifolia* var. *pilosior* (creeping-buttons) produces thin, weak, zigzagging stems and tiny, round, domed leaves with green and silver markings.

Upright *Peperomias*

Upright peperomias have visible stems and generally grow upward, though they become prostrate as the stems become heavier. The best known is *P. obtusifolia* (baby rubber plant), which bears thick stems and waxy, obtuse leaves of varying sizes. Its variegation ranges from light speckling to large zones of yellow or cream. *P. magnoliifolia* has larger leaves. *P. verticillata* produces shiny, sharply pointed leaves in whorls of 3 to 5 along a reddish stem.

Temperature   70° to 75° F days; 55° to 60° F nights. Cooler in winter.

Water   When potting mix feels dry to the touch, water thoroughly. Use tepid water.

Light   Bright indirect light from a south-, east-, or west-facing window. Protect from direct sunlight.

Propagation   In spring and summer, take stem cuttings. You can also divide them.

Potting mix   All-purpose mix; can be supplemented with peat moss.

Repotting   This plant does not like being repotted.

Philodendron hastatum

Philodendron scandens oxycardium

Peperomia obtusifolia

Philodendron 'Red Emerald'

Philodendron selloum

Grooming Pick off yellowed leaves. Prune or pinch upright and trailing ones as needed.

Pests and problems Leaves wilt and drop off suddenly from underwatering. Potting mix should be slightly dry, but do not allow leaves to wilt before watering. Leaves become soft, wilt, and lose color from overwatering, especially in winter.

Philodendrons

No other group of plants has made itself such a prevalent addition to our homes. The leathery, glossy leaves cut in unique shapes, as well as the range of sizes and types—vines, shrubs, and trees—allow you to select one compatible with the look you want to achieve. Originally from South American tropical forests, philodendrons are also strong, tolerant plants that don't need a lot of sunshine.

The 200 different species break down into two types. The "climbers" are most commonly grown in the home. The name is a bit of a misnomer, though: None of them climb very well, so they must be tied to supports or used as hanging plants. Aerial roots extend from their upper leaves to seek nourishment.

The other type, "self-headers," can become enormous plants 6 to 8 feet high. Their leaves, of varying shapes, extend from self-supporting trunks. These are appropriate for large, high-ceiling rooms.

Place the plant in bright light. Feed lightly with each watering all year, more heavily in summer, and provide average indoor humidity levels. About once a month the leaves should be washed. An undersized pot, low temperatures, or poor drainage will cause leaves to yellow and drop. If lower leaves yellow and drop on the climbing types, it's usually natural.

Philodendron bipinnatifidum
Twice-cut philodendron, fiddleleaf philodendron

This plant has large, deeply cut, star-shaped leaves. It is a nonclimbing type, so it needs no supports. A very similar plant is *P. selloum.*

Philodendron 'Black Cardinal'
Black Cardinal philodendron

Shiny deep reddish green leaves typify this plant, which is self-supporting when young but eventually needs staking.

Philodendron hastatum
Spade-leaf philodendron

This lush evergreen climbing vine with aerial roots has deeply veined bright green leaves that take the shape of spearheads 8 to 12 inches long. Older plants produce perfumed tubular blossoms resembling calla lilies.

Philodendron pertusum
See *Monstera deliciosa*

Philodendron 'Pluto'
This nonclimbing type has broad leaves with wavy edges. It can reach 2 feet in height and prefers moderate to bright light.

Philodendron 'Red Emerald'
Red Emerald philodendron

Red stems are topped with spear-shaped bright green, yellow-veined leaves on the Red Emerald philodendron. This is a climber.

Philodendron scandens
Heart-leaf philodendron

This vigorous climber, composed of many long, glossy deep green leaves, is one of the most popular philodendrons grown in the United States. It is also known as *P. oxycardium* or *P. cordatum.* This plant tolerates shade.

Philodendron selloum
Lacy tree philodendron

This is another self-heading, cut-leaf philodendron, very similar to *P. bipinnatifidum.* As the plant ages, the cuts become more pronounced and cause the leaves to ruffle.

Care of Philodendrons

Temperature Average warmth, not less than 55° F in winter.

Water Keep evenly moist but not soggy.

Light Moderate to bright indirect light but no direct sunlight

Propagation Take stem cuttings in summer or layer. Air-layer climbing types. Provide warmth.

Repotting Repot about every 2 to 3 years in spring.

Plectranthus australis

Pilea microphylla

Polyscias fruticosa 'Elegans'

Grooming Place aerial roots in potting mix so that upper leaves can receive nourishment, or tie them to plant supports. Leaves collect dust, so clean periodically.

Pests and problems It is natural for most philodendrons to drop lower leaves.

Pilea
Aluminum-plant, artillery plant, creeping-Charlie

The profuse number of *Pilea* species available and the ease with which they grow make them very popular. Best known is the aluminum-plant, *P. cadierei*, which features fleshy stems and silver-splashed leaves. *P. microphylla*, the artillery plant, sports tiny fernlike leaves and ejects puffs of pollen when disturbed. Both of these varieties are bushy and reach a height of about 12 inches. Two trailing types are *P. depressa*, shiny creeping-Charlie, and *P. nummulariifolia*, hairy creeping-Charlie. Both have small, round leaves.

These fast-growing plants are well known for their ability to withstand neglect,

although with age they tend to become unattractive. To control the spindly growth of older plants, pinch back stems and repot frequently, grow new plants each spring from the easily rooted cuttings. For the fullest look, put several cuttings in one pot.

Pileas require moist air; the small varieties do well in a terrarium. Feed lightly with each watering throughout the growing season.

Temperature 68° to 75° F days; 65° to 68° F nights. Not less than 50° F in winter.

Water Water thoroughly when potting mix becomes dry to the touch. Reduce amount in winter.

Light Bright indirect light or slight shade.

Propagation Stem cuttings root easily.

Repotting Every year in spring.

Grooming Pinch out growing tips to keep plants bushy.

Pests and problems Wilted, discolored leaves result from overwatering. Brown edges on leaves usually develop from too little light or a sudden drop in temperature. Cold air

and wet potting mix in winter will cause leaf drop. However, some leaf shedding in winter is normal. Bare stems should be cut back in spring.

Plectranthus
Swedish ivy

The waxy, leathery leaved bright green trailing member of the Mint family, *P. australis* is commonly known as Swedish ivy, although it is neither from Sweden nor an ivy. The name was attached because it is such a popular hanging and trailing plant in Scandinavia. Spikes of white flowers appear occasionally to complement the foliage. Variegated varieties, such as *P. coleoides, P. oertendahlii,* and *P. purpuratus,* have shadings of silver, purple, and gray-greens, and bear pink or lavender blossoms.

This beautiful trailing plant is fairly tolerant and requires a minimum of care to grow well. Place it in bright light and average indoor humidity levels. Water regularly and feed lightly with each watering while the plant is actively growing.

Temperature 65° to 72° F days; 60° to 70° F nights.

Water Water regularly, keeping mix moist but not soggy.

Light Bright light. Protect from direct sun.

Propagation In spring or summer, take stem cuttings or divide plant. Plantlets start easily.

Repotting Repot every 2 to 3 years.

Grooming Plant tends to get leggy and unattractive with age. Pinch growth tips for a bushier plant.

Polyscias
Aralia, balfour aralia, ming aralia

Aralias are woody shrubs frequently grown indoors for their lacy, often variegated foliage. The leaves of some cultivars are aromatic when crushed or bruised. *P. fruiticosa* (ming aralia) has finely divided leaves and can reach a height of 8 feet. Its cultivar, *P. fruiticosa* 'Elegans', is smaller, with extremely dense foliage. *P. balfouriana* 'Marginata' has leaves edged with

Primula malacoides

Radermachera sinica

white. The leaves of *P. balfouriana* 'Pennockii' are white to light green with green spots. *P. guilfoylei* 'Victoriae' is compact, with deeply divided leaves edged in white.

Give aralias plenty of room. They require moist air; use a humidifier for best results. Feed lightly with each watering throughout the growing season. Prune them frequently to achieve good form.

Temperature 70° to 75° F days; 55° to 60° F nights.

Water Let plant approach dryness, then water thoroughly.

Light Provide at least moderate light but no direct sunlight.

Propagation Take stem cuttings.

Repotting Repot in winter or early spring, as needed.

Grooming Keep to desired height and shape with light pruning or clipping at any time.

Pests and problems Spider mites, scale insects, and mealybugs may be a problem. Will get spindly and weak if light is too low.

Primula

Primrose, fairy primrose, German primrose, Chinese primrose, polyantha primrose

These winter bloomers are one of the best-known gift plants. Colorful flowers grouped in clusters emerge above leafy rosettes from December to April.

Four species especially suited to indoors are *P. malacoides, P. obconica, P. sinensis,* and *P. × polyantha.* The largest is *P. malacoides,* commonly called the fairy primrose. Star-shaped, scented flowers are borne in tiers on tall stalks. *P. obconica* (German primrose) reaches a foot in height and blooms in white, lilac, crimson, and salmon. *P. sinensis* (Chinese primrose) is the primula usually carried by florists. This small plant features delicate, ruffled flowers in a wide range of colors, pink being the most common. *P. × polyantha* (polyantha primrose) has fragrant flowers in white, yellow, pink, red, lavender, purple, and orange. All four primroses have similar care requirements.

A well-lit, cool area such as a sun porch is ideal because primroses like their roots to be cool. Primroses require moist air; use a humidifier for best results. Feed lightly.

Temperature Cool: 55° to 60° F while flowering.

Water Keep constantly moist.

Light Bright indirect light.

Propagation Sow seeds in June or July.

Potting mix All-purpose mix supplemented with lime.

Repotting *P. obconica, P. sinensis,* and *P. × polyantha* can be kept for the following season. Repot and place in a shaded, cool, airy location during the summer. Water sparingly until autumn. Remove yellowed leaves. *P. × polyantha* can also be planted permanently in an outdoor garden.

Grooming Pick off yellow leaves and faded blossoms.

Pests and problems Too much heat will shorten the flowering period, as will failure to remove dead flowers. Crown rot occurs when primroses have been planted too deeply. Leaves will turn yellow with overfeeding.

Radermachera sinica

China-doll

The shiny bright green leaves of the China-doll are doubly compound, giving the plant a delicate, fernlike appearance. It reaches 4 feet in height. In the nursery it is usually treated with a growth retardant; as the effect wears off, the plant will return to its more open natural growth habit. Provide average indoor humidity levels and feed lightly with each watering throughout the growing season.

Temperature 70° to 75° F days; 60° to 65° F nights.

Water Keep evenly moist.

Light Provide 2 to 3 hours of curtain-filtered sunlight in a south, east, or west window.

Propagation Take stem cuttings.

Repotting Repot as necessary.

Grooming Pick off yellowed leaves. Keep to desired height and shape by pinching.

Pests and problems Leaves may dry up if mix dries out between waterings.

Rhododendron (Azalea)

Saintpaulia ionantha

Rhipsalidopsis gaertneri

See *Schlumbergera*

Rhododendron

Azalea, rhododendron

For winter color indoors it's hard to outdo azaleas. Masses of white, pink, or red single or double flowers cover the dark evergreen foliage. When not in flower, they make beautiful foliage plants.

Select plants that are covered with buds just about to open. To keep your plant blooming for several weeks, place it in a cool, brightly lit spot and keep the potting mix very moist. Fertilize lightly with an acid-based fertilizer with each watering while the plant is actively growing or flowering and add trace elements once in spring. Azaleas also require moist air; use a humidifier for best results.

Temperature   Cool: 45° to 60° F.

Water   Keep evenly moist.

Light   Bright indirect light. An eastern or western exposure is best. Can be placed anywhere when blooming.

Propagation   After flowering, when new foliage reaches maturity, root cuttings 2 to 3 inches long from stem tips.

Potting mix   Well drained and acidic: 1 part sphagnum peat moss and 1 part coarse builder's sand.

Repotting   Repot infrequently.

Grooming   Don't discard these plants after they bloom. Snip off dead blossoms and old leaves, trim back branches, and repot in a 1-inch larger pot. Move outside in late spring to a shady spot.

Pests and problems   Spider mites may be a problem. Needs cool temperatures and acid potting mix to rebloom. Brown tips or yellow leaves result from dry air.

Rhoeo Spathacea

See *Tradescantia*

Saintpaulia

African violet

In terms of popularity, these plants are first in any list of favorite flowering plants. No other plant equals their ability to thrive and bloom indoors for months on end.

Rosettes of velvety leaves on short stems surround clusters of flowers in white, and shades of pink, red, violet, purple, yellow, or blue. This plant's compact size makes it perfect for windowsills, small tabletop arrangements, and hanging displays.

There are thousands of named African violets from which to choose. For beginners, it's best to start with varieties that have plain green leaves rather than fancier types, which are not as easy to grow. Some favorites include 'Swifty Thriller', 'Half Moon Bay', and 'Granger's Wonderland'. Consult local experts or plant catalogs to determine varieties you find most appealing.

Despite their reputation for being temperamental, African violets generally are not difficult to grow. Plenty of bright indirect light is the key factor in achieving constant bloom. Supplement with artificial light if the plant stops blooming, especially in winter when the plant receives less than 12 hours of good light a day. An evenly moist potting mix, warm temperatures, high air humidity, and feeding once a month throughout the year are the other important factors for good growth. Keep the air around the plant moist by surrounding the base with moist peat moss or placing it on a humidifying tray. The plants will flower best with only one crown (the area where stems come together and join the roots). Use additional crown growth for rooting new plants.

Recently, miniature varieties have received more attention. Sold in 2½-inch pots, they grow only to be 6 inches across and are true space savers that make wonderful additions to collections, indoor landscapes, terrariums, or miniature greenhouses. Semiminiatures have somewhat smaller leaves and crowns than standards, but their flowers grow to be almost as large. One of the most reliable miniatures is 'Mickey Mouse'. Outstanding semiminiatures include 'Precious Pink', 'Snuggles', and 'Magic Blue'. Popular microminiatures include 'Optimara Rose Quartz' and

Saxifraga stolonifera

Schlumbergera × *buckleyi*

'Optimara Blue Sapphire'. Trailing miniatures and semi-miniatures are also available.

One valuable tip for growing miniatures is to keep the potting mix constantly moist. Many growers use self-watering containers.

Temperature   Average: 72° to 75° F days; 60° to 65° F nights. Keep plants away from cold windowpanes. Sudden changes in temperature are harmful.

Water   Keep the potting mix evenly moist. Use only water that is at room temperature. Avoid wetting foliage: Cold water spots the leaves. Leach potting mix occasionally.

Light   Bright light. Direct sun in winter is fine, but summer sun may be too strong. In general, the more light the better. During the winter, supplement with artificial light so that the plant receives at least 14 hours of light a day.

Propagation   In spring, take leaf cuttings or sow seed.

Potting mix   African violet mix. For a light, porous mix, combine 1 part garden loam,

1 part leaf mold, and 1 part sand.

Repotting   African violets like being slightly pot bound. A pot about one third the width of the plant's spread is a good size.

Grooming   Remove all dead leaves and flowers promptly, stems included. Shape the plant by removing suckers.

Pests and problems   Mushy brown blooms and buds indicate botrytis blight. Pick off diseased parts. Provide good air circulation, avoid high humidity, and reduce amount of nitrogen in the fertilizer.

Yellow rings on the leaf surface are caused by cold water touching foliage.

Crown rot results from an erratic watering routine or severe temperature changes. Discard the plant.

Lack of flowers is probably caused by very dry air or very cold air or inadequate light. Supplement with artificial light. Repotting and moving the plant can also inhibit flowering.

Yellowing leaves result from dry air, too much sun, incorrect watering, or improper fertilizing. Brittle brown

leaves develop from potting mix that is deficient in nutrients. Repot if potting mix is old; fertilize regularly.

Slow growth and leaves curled downward indicate that the temperature is too low. Soft foliage and few flowers can be caused by temperatures that are too high. Brown-edged leaves and small flowers are a result of low humidity.

Saxifraga stolonifera
Strawberry-geranium, strawberry-begonia

Saxifraga stolonifera is neither a geranium nor a begonia; its common names come from its shape, resembling geranium leaves, and the colors of the foliage, resembling begonias. One variegated cultivar, *S. stolonifera* 'Tricolor', is available, but is not as easy to maintain as the species.

Strawberry-geraniums are best suited for ground covers or hanging containers. They divide quickly, sending out runners that form plantlets. In summer, small white flowers appear on long stalks above the foliage. Strawberry-geraniums do well in average

indoor humidity levels. Feed lightly with each watering when the plant is actively growing.

Temperature   60° to 65° F days; 50° to 55° F nights.

Water   Let plant approach dryness, then water thoroughly.

Light   Place in a bright, indirectly lit, south-, east-, or west-facing window.

Propagation   Divide an old specimen, or remove plantlets or rooted side shoots as they form.

Repotting   Cut back and repot each year when flowering stops.

Grooming   Cut flower stalks if you wish.

Pests and problems   Leaves will scorch if the plant is in a draft or dry air.

Schlumbergera
Schlumbergera, Christmas cactus, Thanksgiving cactus, holiday cactus, Easter cactus

The unusual stems and timely seasonal blossoms of these commonly grown houseplants are both delightful and fascinating. The old favorite,

Sinningia speciosa

Soleirolia soleirolii

S. ✕ *buckleyi* (also called *S. bridgesii, Zygocactus truncatus,* and *Z. bridgesii*), or Christmas cactus, features striking, arched bright green branches made up of smooth, flat, scalloped, 1½-inch-long joints. The tubular, 3-inch-long flowers in a wide range of colors appear at Christmastime.

S. truncata (Thanksgiving cactus) flowers earlier in winter. Its stem joints are longer and narrower than the later-blooming Schlumbergeras. Its flowers appear in shades of red and white.

The Easter cactus, *Rhipsalidopsis gaertneri* (also known as *S. gaertneri*), is often confused with *S.* ✕ *buckleyi,* but this plant droops less and the stems and joints sport upright or horizontal, sharply tipped scarlet flowers at Eastertime, and sometimes again in early fall. Cultivars in shades of pink and red are also available.

Schlumbergeras are native to the jungles of South America. They require a rich, porous potting mix and average to high indoor humidity levels. Keep the potting mix moist,

and feed lightly with each watering when the plant is actively growing or flowering. The plants do well in a cool, bright window. During the summer you can move them outdoors into partial shade. Budding results from short days during October and November or cool, dry conditions. To provide this, place your plants outdoors for a time during the fall.

Temperature To set flower buds, 60° to 65° F days and 40° to 45° F nights. Once buds set, 70° to 75° F days and 60° to 70° F nights.

Water Keep evenly moist but not soggy when plant is actively growing and flowering. Allow to dry between waterings when the plant rests.

Light Bright indirect light. Western or northern exposure is best.

Propagation From seed, or stem cuttings when not in flower. Place stem sections in moist vermiculite.

Potting mix African violet mix or 1 part potting mix, 2 parts leaf mold, and 1 part perlite.

Repotting Repot infrequently.

Grooming Prune after flowering, if needed.

Pests and problems Spider mites may be a problem.

Sinningia speciosa
Gloxinia, florist's gloxinia

These velvety-leaved Brazilian Gesneriad family members have bell-shaped flowers with ruffled edges that are borne in clusters atop long stems. Some miniature sinningias have 1½-inch leaves and inch-long flowers that bloom the year around. In practice, growers tend to call the large-flowered, bell-shaped *S. speciosa* species *florist's gloxinias,* and the species and miniature hybrids *sinningias.*

Gloxinias need humidity, full sun in winter, and bright light in summer. Keep the potting mix moist, but not too wet. After blooming ceases and leaf growth reaches a standstill, gradually withhold water until stems and leaves die down; put the plant in a cool, dark, mouseproof place for 2 to 4 months while the

tuber rests. Water sparingly until new growth appears, then repot into fresh mix, move into light and warmth, and provide moisture. While gloxinias are growing, feed lightly with each watering.

Temperature 65° to 70° F days; 60° to 70° F nights.

Water Keep evenly moist while growing and flowering. Do not allow to dry out. Do not water crowns. Use tepid water.

Light Bright indirect light. A southern or western exposure is best.

Propagation From seed or from leaf or stem cuttings rooted in damp sand or perlite.

Potting mix African violet mix.

Repotting Repot when the plant resumes growth after rest periods.

Grooming Remove faded rosettes and yellowed leaves. Handle carefully; the brittle leaves break off easily.

Pests and problems Florist's gloxinias do not bloom all year long. After blooming allow them to rest for 2 to 4 months. Will not bloom if light is too low.

Spathiphyllum 'Mauna Loa'

Streptocarpus

Soleirolia soleirolii
Baby's tears

Often sold as *Helxine soleirolii*, baby's tears is a compact creeper composed of tiny, delicate, rounded leaves on thin, trailing stems. The plant grows thick and dense and makes a good terrarium ground cover.

This plant loves humidity and grows rapidly in moist, greenhouselike conditions or terrariums. Feed lightly with each watering all through the year, more heavily in summer.

Temperature 70° F days; 55° to 60° F nights.

Water Keep potting mix moist. Will not tolerate dry potting mix.

Light Bright indirect light. Northern or eastern exposure is best. Will grow in shade.

Propagation By division or by pressing stem cuttings into potting mix.

Repotting Repot at any time.

Grooming Keep to desired height and shape with light pruning or clipping at any time.

Spathiphyllum
Peace-lily, spatheflower, white anthurium, snowflower

The distinctive flower of *Spathiphyllum* evokes a feeling for its common name, the peace-lily. The spathe is a pure white bract that encloses the true flowers. Sometimes more than 4 inches wide and 6 inches long, it unfurls to form a softly curved backdrop for the central column of these closely set tiny flowers. The fragrant blossom clearly resembles its relative, anthurium. Spoon-shaped leaves on long stalks surround the flower and mirror its shape.

When not in flower, *Spathiphyllum* makes an attractive foliage plant, especially in a shady location. Choose the plants by size: *S.* 'Clevelandii' (white anthurium) grows to a height of 2 feet. *S. floribundum* (snowflower) has leaves less than a foot tall. The largest of these three, *S.* 'Mauna Loa', reaches 3 feet. They bloom in spring and sometimes in autumn. After a few weeks the white spathe turns pale green.

This is one of the easiest large-flowering plants to grow, especially under limited light conditions. All that is needed to bring this plant to bloom is a few hours of bright indirect light daily, normal to warm house temperatures, regular watering, and light feeding with each watering while the plant is actively growing or flowering. Cold drafts will harm the plant, and the surrounding air should be moist, so place the pot on a humidifying tray or fill it with moist peat moss.

Temperature 65° to 75° F days; 60° to 68° F nights.

Water During the growing period, keep well-draining potting mix moist. Water less frequently in winter.

Light Moderate light; this plant can survive and bloom in the shade.

Propagation Easily done by division or seed.

Potting mix All-purpose mix with sphagnum moss added.

Repotting Best done in February or March, but usually not necessary on a yearly basis.

Grooming Cut flower stalks if you wish. Remove old leaves as the plant goes dormant. Wash leaves occasionally.

Streptocarpus
Cape primrose

Commonly known as the cape primrose, *Streptocarpus* is a relative of the African violet and gloxinia and can be grown under similar conditions.

Arching flower stalks, each bearing between two to more than a dozen trumpetlike blooms, are borne directly on stemless, straplike leaves similar to those of primroses. Many colorful varieties in white, pink, red, violet, or blue are available. The 'Wiesmoor' hybrids reach 6 to 8 inches and bear 1½- to 3-inch flowers. 'Nymph' hybrids grow 10 to 12 inches high with 1- to 2-inch flowers that bloom from spring to fall. 'Mount Olympus' hybrids, with 1-inch flowers, are more compact and bloom the year around.

Streptocarpus prefers a cooler environment than African violets and especially enjoys a temperature drop at night. Raise it in shallow pots

Succulent: Agave americana

Succulent: Beaucarnea recurvata

Succulent: Ceropegia woodii

Succulent: Echeveria elegans

Succulent: Haworthia

with good drainage and where the air is humid. In summer, a north-facing window away from midday sun is ideal. Water freely during the flowering season and feed lightly with each watering.

Temperature 65° to 70° F days; 60° to 65° F nights.

Water Keep moist during the growing period and provide good drainage. Allow to dry out between waterings at other times.

Light Protect from direct sun but provide plenty of indirect light. Supplement with artificial light.

Propagation Easily done from leaf cuttings.

Potting mix All-purpose mix or 2 parts peat moss, 1 part all-purpose mix, and 1 part sharp sand or perlite.

Repotting Not necessary very often.

Grooming Pick off yellowed leaves and trim back those with brown tips. Cut flower stalks after the last bloom has faded.

Pests and problems Too little light causes leaves and flowers to droop. Will wilt if kept too hot or too moist. If

leaves go limp, yet the potting mix seems moist, keep the plant drier than usual and place it in a shady spot until it recovers.

Succulents

A succulent is a plant that stores water in its stems or leaves. These plants have mastered the art of water conservation.

Succulents are usually easy to care for and are a good starting point for beginning gardeners. Despite the many different types of succulent plants, they require generally the same care. They need a porous, well-draining potting mix, lots of sunshine, good air circulation, and plenty of water. These plants do well in low humidity levels. Feed lightly with each watering while the plants are actively growing or flowering. During the winter they prefer to remain dormant in a cool, dry environment. Do not feed at this time if you want your plants to bloom the following season. In summer, revitalize the plants by moving them outdoors.

Agave
Agave, painted century plant, century plant

These succulents feature straplike leaves in rosettes that grow from 3 inches to 8 feet when mature. *A. victoriae-reginae*, the painted century plant, has dark green leaves edged in creamy white. *A. americana*, the century plant, has large triangular leaves with saw-toothed edges. White to yellow-green flowers are borne on long stalks from the center of the rosette only when the plant is very old. Variegated varieties of *A. americana* are also available. All agaves flower only once, after which the individual rosette dies. The agave requires a large pot and plenty of water and fertilizer during its active growing season.

Beaucarnea
Bottle palm, elephantfoot tree, ponytail-palm

Outdoors the bottle palm eventually grows into a tree 20 feet tall, but as a houseplant it will stay a manageable size. *B. recurvata*, the elephantfoot tree or ponytail-palm, is most often

distinguished by the base of the gray-brown trunk, which resembles a large onion. Long, thin green leaves arch out all around the apex of the stem, creating a fountainlike effect.

Ceropegia woodii
Rosary vine, hearts-entangled

The rosary vine sports trailing stems of small, heart-shaped dark green leaves marbled with white or silver. Tiny flowers with bulbous bases and black petals joined at the tips appear all along the vines. Most bloom in summer, but a few appear in spring and fall. Tubers periodically appear along the stems, and new growth starts from these.

Rosary vine makes an attractive, especially interesting hanging plant for interiors. Give it more water than you would other succulents.

Crassula argentea
Jade plant, baby jade

This compact, treelike succulent has stout, branching limbs with oblong, fleshy leaves, 1 to 2 inches long. Its star-shaped flowers bloom in winter. In direct sun, the smooth, leathery dark green leaves become

Succulent: Sansevieria trifasciata

Succulent: Lithops

Succulent: Kalanchoe blossfeldiana

Succulent: Sedum morganianum

Succulent: Senecio rowleyanus

tinged with red. This popular plant ranges in height from 1 to 5 feet, with many shapes and forms.

Echeveria

Echeveria, hen and chicks, pearl echeveria

All echeverias have a rosette form in common though their varied leaf color ranges from pale green through deep purple. Many are luminous pink in full sun. *E. elegans,* hen and chicks or the pearl echeveria, forms a tight rosette of small whitish green leaves. Rose-colored flowers tipped with yellow are borne on pink stems in spring or summer. These are attractive in dish gardens.

Echeverias do well with more water, fertilizer, and a richer potting mix than most succulents. Exposure to light directly affects the intensity of the foliage color. Cut down and reroot if stems become leggy.

Haworthia

All haworthias are excellent indoor plants. Although they grow in moderate light, bright indirect light improves their foliage color and texture. The leaves of most species are thick and form rosettes on stemless plants. They flower at different times, depending on the species. The flowers are small and borne in clusters on long stems. After flowering, the plants may go dormant and will need repotting.

Kalanchoe

Kalanchoe, felt-plant, Christmas kalanchoe, flaming-katy, pandaplant, devil's backbone

One of the more popular succulents, kalanchoes are grown for both their flowers and foliage. *K. beharensis,* the felt-plant, features large triangular leaves, covered with brown felt, that curve and wave to create a busy look. Pink flowers appear in spring. *K. blossfeldiana,* the Christmas kalanchoe or flaming-katy, produces brilliant heads of scarlet, pink, yellow, or orange flowers on thin stems up to 15 inches high. Oval shiny green leaves are tinged with red. *K. tomentosa,* the pandaplant, grows to 15 inches. Plump leaves covered with furlike silvery hairs

branch from the central stem. The pointed leaves are tipped with rusty brown bumps. Indoors, this species rarely flowers. *K. daigremontiana,* the devil's backbone, has plantlets on its leaves but also rarely flowers indoors.

Lithops

Living stones

Often called living stones because of its close resemblance both in shape and coloring to small rocks, *Lithops* grows in stemless clumps of paired leaves approximately 1 to 2 inches in diameter. In November, dandelion-shaped yellow to white flowers emerge from between the leaves. Extreme care must be taken in watering or rot will set in.

Sansevieria

Sansevieria, snakeplant, mother-in-law's-tongue

One of the toughest of all indoor plants is *S. trifasciata.* From a central rosette emerge erect, lance-shaped leaves, dark green in color. Horizontal bands of gray-green create a striking pattern similar to the coloring of an exotic snake. *S. trifasciata* 'Laurentii' has

wide yellow stripes along the leaf edges. Dwarf varieties include *S. trifasciata* 'Hahnii' and *S.trifasciata* 'Golden Hahnii'.

Given proper care, sansevieria will become a showy accent for any indoor decor. Place in a brightly lit, warm spot and water regularly when the potting mix becomes dry. Overwatering will cause root rot. Feed lightly with a low-nitrogen fertilizer in spring and summer. Continue feeding, even more lightly, through fall and winter for plants that grow actively the year around. Dry air does no harm, but keep the plant out of drafts.

Sedum morganianum

Donkey's-tail, burro's-tail

This sedum, commonly called donkey's-tail or burro's-tail, is a trailing, slow-growing succulent. Light gray to blue-green leaves are ½ to 1 inch long, oval, and plump. The 3- to 4-foot-long trailing stems, covered with clusters of these leaves, create a braided or ropelike effect. This plant is ideal for hanging containers. Locate it where it won't be disturbed, because leaflets break

Succulent: Yucca pendula glauca

Syngonium podophyllum

off easily. The powdery bluish dust that covers the leaves is called *bloom*.

Senecio rowleyanus
String-of-beads

The string-of-beads has hanging stems that bear ½-inch spherical leaves. These unusual leaves look like light green beads with pointed tips and have a single translucent band across them. Small white flowers appear in winter.

Yucca

Though more commonly grown outdoors, yuccas may be used indoors as a large, dramatic accent plant. The thick, sword-like leaves have sharp tips that can puncture the skin. Many plants have a canelike trunk with whorls of foliage at the end. Side shoots form occasionally. *Y. elephantipes* has wide dark green leaves 4 feet long. Canes taken from sections of large stock plants will quickly produce a floor-sized specimen.

Care of Succulents

Temperature   70° to 80° F days; 65° F nights.

Water   Water thoroughly when the potting mix feels dry a half-inch below the surface; discard drainage.

Light   Full sun. A south-facing exposure on a windowsill is fine. *Sansevieria* does well in low light. Plants moved outside should be placed in shade.

Propagation   Cuttings and offsets root easily. Dust the exposed cut with fungicide. Dry the offset or cutting for a few days until a callus is formed on the wound, then plant in appropriate potting mix and keep barely moist. Many species can also be propagated by leaf cuttings.

Potting mix   Cactus mix or 1 part coarse sand or pumice, 1 part all-purpose mix, and 1 part leaf mold.

Repotting   Repot only every 3 to 4 years, when essential, in a shallow pot.

Grooming   Cut off faded flower stalks.

Pests and problems   Root rot results from soggy potting mix. Stem and leaf rot come from cool, damp air. Leaves wilt and discolor from too much water, especially in winter. Dry brown spots indicate

underwatering. Soft brown spots indicate leaf spot disease.

Syngonium podophyllum
Syngonium, arrowhead vine

This plant closely resembles its relatives, the climbing philodendrons, both in appearance and care. An unusual feature of syngonium is the change that occurs in the leaf shape as the plant ages. Young leaves are 3 inches long, arrow shaped, and borne at the ends of erect stalks. They are dark green, often with bold variegation in silvery white or pink. With age the leaves become lobed and the stems acquire a climbing habit. Eventually each leaf fans out into several leaflets; older leaves sport up to 11 leaflets and usually lose their variegation. All stages of leaf development appear simultaneously on mature plants.

Arrowhead vines do best in a warm, moist environment, protected from direct sunlight. Older climbing stems require support. To retain the juvenile

leaf form and variegation, prune off the climbing stems and aerial roots as they appear. Fertilize lightly with each watering while the plant is actively growing.

Temperature   Average warmth: at least 60° F in winter.

Water   Keep the potting mix barely moist at all times. Water less in winter and avoid overwatering.

Light   Bright indirect light away from direct sun, especially for solid green types.

Propagation   In spring or summer, take stem cuttings.

Repotting   Every 2 to 3 years in spring.

Grooming   Pinch off long stems at any time to increase branching and encourage more young, variegated leaves.

Pests and problems   Older climbing stems may require support.

Tolmiea menziesii
Piggyback plant, mother-of-thousands

This popular plant is noted for its unusual leaf growth: The hairy bright green leaves send

Tolmiea menziesii

Tradescantia zebrina

out tiny new plantlets at the junction of the leaf and stem, giving the plant its common name of piggyback plant. Because so many new plants form, it's also sometimes called mother-of-thousands.

These easy-to-grow plants do fine in a cool, well-ventilated spot. Keep in average to high indoor humidity levels; keep the potting mix moist; and feed every 2 months. This plant tolerates shade.

Temperature 55° to 70° F days; 40° to 55° F nights.

Water Keep the potting mix evenly moist.

Light Bright indirect light but will tolerate lower light levels.

Propagation Leaf cuttings with plantlets root easily any time.

Repotting Any time when plant becomes overcrowded.

Grooming Pinch off wilted leaves immediately. Prune to shape.

Pests and problems Brittle brown leaves signal spider mite attack. Treat immediately. Plant was probably too hot and dry.

Tradescantia

Striped inch-plant, wandering-Jew, purple-heart, Moses-in-the-cradle, boat-lily, oyster plant, inch-plant, spiderwort

Wandering-Jew, inch-plant, spiderwort—these are all common names for the popular and easily grown houseplants in the spiderwort family. Although traditionally they belong to different genera, they have such similar needs that many are being reclassified under the genera *Tradescantia*.

Tradescantias have boat-shaped leaves of varying lengths borne alternately along trailing stems. All of them flower seasonally, but most are grown strictly for their colorful or variegated foliage. They work well in hanging containers or as trailing plants on shelves.

These plants are easy to care for and grow rapidly. Place in a bright spot with direct sun; an eastern or western exposure is best. Allow the potting mix to dry between waterings and keep in average indoor humidity levels. Feed lightly with each watering while the plant is actively growing.

Tradescantia, the striped inch-plant or wandering-Jew, is variegated with white or cream bands. Some of the most popular forms are *T. albiflora* 'Albovittata', *T. blossfeldiana* 'Variegata', and *T. fluminensis* 'Variegata'. *T. sillamontana* bears entirely green leaves, which are covered in woolly white hair.

T. pallida, the purple-heart (formerly known as *Setcreasea pallida*), is slower growing than most tradescantias and needs more light to bring out the attractive deep purple that gives it its name.

T. spathacea, formerly *Rhoeo spathacea*, gets its common names of Moses-in-the-cradle, boat-lily, and oyster plant from the small white blooms that appear within cupped bracts at the base of the terminal leaves on the shoots. The foliage is striking: green on top and deep purple or maroon beneath.

T. zebrina, formerly *Zebrina pendula* and commonly known as wandering-Jew, has shiny green leaves with broad, iridescent silver bands and purple undersides. Among the various variegated forms, *T. zebrina* 'Quadricolor' is the most colorful, being heavily striped with white and pink.

Callisia elegans, also called the striped inch-plant, is often mistaken for *Tradescantia*. Its leaves are olive green with white stripes.

Temperature 65° to 70° F days; 50° to 55° F nights.

Water Water thoroughly when the potting mix feels dry. Water the plants less often in winter.

Light Bright indirect light but no direct sunlight. *T. pallida* prefers some direct sunlight.

Propagation Take stem cuttings any time. Divide *T. spathacea*.

Repotting Each spring when plant is crowded.

Grooming Pinch back to encourage bushy growth.

Pests and problems Will get spindly and weak if light is too low.

Zebrina pendula

See *Tradescantia*

Index of Common Names

If a plant's common and botanical names are the same, the plant name will not be on this list. For more detailed information, see the Index at the back of the book.

A centerpiece of marigolds, lobelia, ivy, and sweet alyssum echoes the colors found throughout this dining room.

Houseplant Societies and Magazines

For further information on any plants mentioned in this book, there is no better source than the plant society that is devoted to its culture. Most of these societies offer regular publications, seed or spore banks, round-robins, conventions, and many other activities to their members. If you find yourself developing a special interest in a specific plant group, contact the society that interests you so that it can send you more details on membership and activities. With any query, please make a habit of including a dollar and a self-addressed, stamped envelope (or, for international correspondence, a self-addressed business-sized envelope and two international reply coupons) for postage and handling.

African Violet Society of America, Inc.
P.O. Box 3609
Beaumont, TX 77704

African Violet Society of Canada
1573 Arbordale Avenue
Victoria, British Columbia
V8N 5J1

American Begonia Society
157 Monument Road
Rio Dell, CA 95562-1617

American Bonsai Society
P.O. Box 238
Keene, NH 03431

American Fuchsia Society
County Fair Building
9th Avenue at Lincoln Way
San Francisco, CA 94122

American Ginger Society
P.O. Box 100
Archer, FL 32618

American Gloxinia and Gesneriad Society, Inc.
128 West 58th Street
New York, NY 10019

American Hibiscus Society
P.O. Box 321540
Cocoa Beach, FL 32932-1540

American Ivy Society
P.O. Box 520
West Carrollton, OH 45449-0520

American Orchid Society
6000 S. Olive Avenue
West Palm Beach, FL 33405

American Plant Life Society (bulbs)
P.O. Box 985
National City, CA 92050

American Poinsettia Society
P.O. Box 706
Mission, TX 785672-1256

Bonsai Clubs International
2636 W. Mission Road, #277
Tallahassee, FL 32304

The British Cactus and Succulent Society
43 Dewer Drive
Sheffield, England S7 2GR

Bromeliad Society, Inc.
2488 E. 49th Street
Tulsa, OK 47105

Cactus and Succulent Society of America
P.O. Box 35034
Des Moines, IA 50315-0301

Canadian Orchid Society
128 Adelaide Street
Winnipeg, Manitoba
R3A 0W5

The Cryptanthus Society
2355 Rusk
Beaumont, TX 77702

The Cycad Society
1161 Phyllis Court
Mountain View, CA 94040

Cymbidium Society of America
6881 Wheeler Avenue
Westminster, CA 92683

Epiphyllum Society of America
P.O Box 1395
Monrovia, CA 91017

Epiphytic Plant Study Group
1 Belvedere Park
Great Crosby, Lancashire, L23 0SP
England

Gesneriad Hybridizers Association
2206 E. 66th Street
Brooklyn, NY 11234

Gesneriad Society International
1109 Putnam Boulevard
Wallingford, PA 19086

Hobby Greenhouse Association
8 Glen Terrace
Bedford, MA 01730-2048

HousePlant Magazine
P.O. Box 1638
Elkins, WV 26241-9909

Hoya Society International
P.O. Box 54271
Atlanta, GA 30308

Hydroponic Society of America
P.O. Box 6067
Concord, CA 94553

Indoor Citrus and Rare Fruit Society
490 Spring Grove Road
Hollister, CA 94023-9366

Indoor Gardening Society of America, Inc.
944 South Monroe Road
Tallmadge, OH 44278

International Aroid Society
P.O. Box 43-1853
Miami, FL 33143

International Asclepiad Society
10 Moorside Terrace, Driglington
Bradford, England BD11 1HX

International Carnivorous Plant Society
Fullerton Arboretum, California State University
Fullerton, CA 92634

International Geranium Society
4610 Druid Street
Los Angeles, CA 90032-3202

International Hoya Association
P.O. Box 5130
Central Point, OR 97502

The International Palm Society
P.O. Box 368
Lawrence, KS 66044

International Tropical Fern Society
8720 W. 34th Street
Miami, FL 33165

Los Angeles International Fern Society
P.O. Box 90943
Pasadena, CA 91109-0943

National Fuchsia Society
11507 E. 187th Street
Artesia, CA 90701

Pacific Orchid Society
P.O. Box 1091
Honolulu, HI 96808

Peperomia Society International
5240 W. 20th Street
Vero Beach, FL 32960

The Plumeria Society of America, Inc.
P.O Box 22791
Houston, TX 77227-2791

Rare Pit and Plant Council
251 W. 11th Street
New York, NY 10014

Saintpaulia and Houseplant Society
33 Common Rd.
Langley, Slough
England SL3 8JZ

Saintpaulia International
1650 Cherry Hill Road
State College, PA 16803

U.S. Measure and Metric Measure Conversion Chart

		Formulas for Exact Measures			Rounded Measures for Quick Reference		
	Symbol	When you know:	Multiply by:	To find:			
Mass	oz	ounces	28.35	grams	1 oz		= 30 g
(Weight)	lb	pounds	0.45	kilograms	4 oz		= 115 g
	g	grams	0.035	ounces	8 oz		= 225 g
	kg	kilograms	2.2	pounds	16 oz	= 1 lb	= 450 g
					32 oz	= 2 lb	= 900 g
					36 oz	= 2¼ lb	= 1000 g (1 kg)
Volume	pt	pints	0.47	liters	1 c	= 8 oz	= 250 ml
	qt	quarts	0.95	liters	2 c (1 pt)	= 16 oz	= 500 ml
	gal	gallons	3.785	liters	4 c (1 qt)	= 32 oz	= 1 liter
	ml	milliliters	0.034	fluid ounces	4 qt (1 gal)	= 128 oz	= 3¾ liter
Length	in.	inches	2.54	centimeters	⅜ in.	= 1 cm	
	ft	feet	30.48	centimeters	1 in.	= 2.5 cm	
	yd	yards	0.9144	meters	2 in.	= 5 cm	
	mi	miles	1.609	kilometers	2½ in.	= 6.5 cm	
	km	kilometers	0.621	miles	12 in. (1 ft)	= 30 cm	
	m	meters	1.094	yards	1 yd	= 90 cm	
	cm	centimeters	0.39	inches	100 ft	= 30 m	
					1 mi	= 1.6 km	
Temperature	°F	Fahrenheit	⅝ (after subtracting 32)	Celsius	32° F	= 0° C	
	°C	Celsius	⅝ (then add 32)	Fahrenheit	212° F	= 100° C	
Area	in.²	square inches	6.452	square centimeters	1 in.²	= 6.5 cm²	
	ft²	square feet	929.0	square centimeters	1 ft²	= 930 cm²	
	yd²	square yards	8361.0	square centimeters	1 yd²	= 8360 cm²	
	a.	acres	0.4047	hectares	1 a.	= 4050 m²	